**Understanding
American History**

The
Relocation of
the American
Indian

Don Nardo

Bruno Leone
Series Consultant

ReferencePoint
Press®

San Diego, CA

© 2015 ReferencePoint Press, Inc.
Printed in the United States

For more information, contact:
ReferencePoint Press, Inc.
PO Box 27779
San Diego, CA 92198
www.ReferencePointPress.com

LIBRARY OF CONGRESS CATALOGING-IN-PUBLICATION DATA

Nardo, Don, 1947–
  The relocation of the American Indian / by Don Nardo.
    pages cm. -- (Understanding American history)
  Includes bibliographical references and index.
  ISBN-13: 978-1-60152-646-5 (hardback)
  ISBN-10: 1-60152-646-6 (hardback)
1. Indian Removal, 1813-1903--Juvenile literature. 2. Indians of North America--Government relations--Juvenile literature. 3. Indians of North America--Crimes against--Juvenile literature.
4. Indian reservations--United States--History--Juvenile literature. I. Title.
  E98.R4N37   2015
  323.1197--dc23
                                                   2013042265

Contents

Foreword

America's Puritan ancestors—convinced that their adopted country was blessed by God and would eventually rise to worldwide prominence—proclaimed their new homeland the shining "city upon a hill." The nation that developed since those first hopeful words were uttered has clearly achieved prominence on the world stage and it has had many shining moments but its history is not without flaws. The history of the United States is a virtual patchwork of achievements and blemishes. For example, America was originally founded as a New World haven from the tyranny and persecution prevalent in many parts of the Old World. Yet the colonial and federal governments in America took little or no action against the use of slave labor by the southern states until the 1860s, when a civil war was fought to eliminate slavery and preserve the federal union.

In the decades before and after the Civil War, the United States underwent a period of massive territorial expansion; through a combination of purchase, annexation, and war, its east–west borders stretched from the Atlantic to the Pacific Oceans. During this time, the Industrial Revolution that began in eighteenth-century Europe found its way to America, where it was responsible for considerable growth of the national economy. The United States was now proudly able to take its place in the Western Hemisphere's community of nations as a worthy economic and technological partner. Yet America also chose to join the major western European powers in a race to acquire colonial empires in Africa, Asia, and the islands of the Caribbean and South Pacific. In this scramble for empire, foreign territories were often peacefully annexed but military force was readily used when needed, as in the Philippines during the Spanish-American War of 1898.

Toward the end of the nineteenth century and concurrent with America's ambitions to acquire colonies, its vast frontier and expanding industrial base provided both land and jobs for a new and ever-growing wave of immigrants from southern and eastern Europe. Although America had always encouraged immigration, these newcomers—Italians, Greeks, and eastern European Jews, among others—were seen as different from the vast majority of earlier immigrants, most of whom were from northern and western Europe. The presence of these newcomers was treated as a matter of growing concern, which in time evolved into intense opposition. Congress boldly and with calculated prejudice set out to create a barrier to curtail the influx of unwanted nationalities and ethnic groups to America's shores. The outcome was the National Origins Act, passed in 1924. That law severely reduced immigration to the United States from southern and eastern Europe. Ironically, while this was happening, the Statue of Liberty stood in New York Harbor as a visible and symbolic beacon lighting the way for people of *all* nationalities and ethnicities seeking sanctuary in America.

Unquestionably, the history of the United States has not always mirrored that radiant beacon touted by the early settlers. As often happens, reality and dreams tend to move in divergent directions. However, the story of America also reveals a people who have frequently extended a helping hand to a weary world and who have displayed a ready willingness—supported by a flexible federal constitution—to take deliberate and effective steps to correct injustices, past and present. America's private and public philanthropy directed toward other countries during times of natural disasters (such as the contributions of financial and human resources to assist Haiti following the January 2010 earthquake) and the legal right to adopt amendments to the US Constitution (including the Thirteenth Amendment freeing the slaves and the Nineteenth Amendment granting women the right to vote) are examples of the nation's generosity and willingness to acknowledge and reverse wrongs.

With objectivity and candor, the titles selected for the Understanding American History series portray the many sides of America, depicting both its shining moments and its darker hours. The series strives to help readers achieve a wider understanding and appreciation of the American experience and to encourage further investigation into America's evolving character and founding principles.

Important Events of the
Indian Relocation

1609
Two years after English settlers establish Jamestown in Virginia, they begin to consider seizing land from the local Indians.

1825
President James Monroe declares that Indians and whites cannot live together in the same society.

1835
President Andrew Jackson delivers an ultimatum to the Georgia Cherokees saying that they must vacate their lands.

1803
The United States buys the Louisiana Territory, a huge chunk of territory on which it will later settle Indians removed from their lands.

1600 ••• **1800** **1825**

1778
The newly formed United States signs its first Indian treaty, with the Delaware tribe; it is an agreement the government will soon break.

1813
Tecumseh, an Indian leader who had attempted to unite all the eastern tribes against US intrusion into their lands, dies.

1830
Congress passes the Indian Removal Act, which allows the US president to decide which tribes should be deprived of their lands.

1836
The US Army begins marching the remaining eastern Creek Indians westward to lands beyond the Mississippi River.

TECUMSEH.

1837
A US Army general violates a flag of truce by arresting the Seminole chief who arrives to negotiate with him under that truce.

2012
Conditions on some Indian reservations remain unmodernized, including 14 percent of homes without electricity.

1849
A gold rush in California sets in motion a westward migration of white prospectors and settlers that passes directly through Indian lands.

1877
The Nez Percés, led by Chief Joseph, escape their reservation and attempt to flee to Canada.

1924
Congress grants American Indians US citizenship and allows them to leave their reservations without a special pass.

1850 **1875** **1900** ••• **2000**

1838
The Cherokee removal known as the Trail of Tears begins.

1890
At Wounded Knee Creek in South Dakota, US soldiers massacre 153 Indians, marking the last major armed encounter of the Indian Wars.

1973
Indian activists take over the village of Wounded Knee, South Dakota, to protest US failure to uphold its Indian treaties.

1861
The American Civil War begins; many relocated Indians take sides and their lands end up devastated.

1934
Congress passes the Indian Reorganization Act, which calls for better treatment of Indians.

Introduction

The Defining Characteristics of Indian Removal

In the early decades of the nineteenth century, the US government forcibly removed numerous Native American tribes from the country's eastern states. In long, often merciless marches in which many of the Indians died, soldiers relocated them in selected regions of the American West. There, the displaced peoples faced a host of new and unexpected dangers and dilemmas that further robbed them of their dignity and in some cases their lives.

The removal and relocation of many eastern Indian tribes in the 1830s and 1840s was destructive and by today's standards unethical. But it was perfectly legal—because the US government passed laws that provided for and sanctioned the policy.

By the early 1800s the act of uprooting and relocating Native Americans had been going on for centuries, ever since the first Europeans had landed in North America in the early 1600s. In 1830 Congress simply formalized the process by passing the Indian Removal Act. Those it aimed to get rid of then occupied only a few tiny islands of Indian culture in a vast sea of white society that stretched from the Atlantic Seaboard westward to the Mississippi River.

That same removal policy continued without interruption into the early 1850s. In the forty-odd years that followed, white civilization rolled like a gargantuan steamroller over the tribes living in the Great

8

Plains and the mountain ranges of the West. The few Indians who survived this human catastrophe ended up on remote reservations on the fringes of American society.

The Europeans Superior?

No matter when it occurred over the centuries, Indian removal had certain defining characteristics. One of the more obvious was the ardent arrogance of those who instigated it. The first white settlers who arrived in what would later become the US Northeast believed that they occupied the very pinnacle of humanity. Their rationale was that they came from Europe, which was composed of well-organized nations that were highly developed from a technological and material standpoint. They had towns and cities that featured towering cathedrals, massive palaces, and other imposing buildings made of stone and brick. Also, those sprawling urban centers and countless farms and forests with well-defined boundaries were interconnected by complex road systems. In addition, the Europeans had large, standing national armies and navies that employed the world's most advanced weapons, including cannons.

When they landed in America, the European settlers found immense stretches of what appeared to be virgin forests, meadows, and mountains. More importantly, these lands were largely undeveloped, at least by European standards. With the exception of small scattered villages, the local inhabitants—the so-called Indians—had no formal towns and cities. Nor did they recognize any well-defined property boundaries or possess guns or other advanced technology.

These factors combined to make the Indians appear primitive and inferior in European eyes. Thinking themselves far and away superior, the white settlers arrogantly fell back on centuries of European law and custom that they felt gave them the right to seize and develop American lands. Typical justification came from legal experts like Swiss jurist Emmerich de Vattel. He argued that the Indians' vast unsettled and undeveloped territories "cannot be accounted a true and legal possession. And the people of Europe, too closely pent up at home, finding land of which the savages stood in no particular need, and of which they made

Indian relocation began with the tribes of the east but eventually spread across the Great Plains and the mountain ranges of the West to envelope tribes such as the Sioux, pictured here in the 1880s in Wyoming.

no actual and constant use, were lawfully entitled to take possession of it, and settle it with colonies."[1]

Arrogance, Racism, and Greed

Growing partly out of the arrogance of the early white settlers was a nasty streak of racism, which became another defining characteristic of Indian removal. The white view was that the Native Americans were not only culturally inferior, but also physically inferior because they were nonwhite. Indians were not the only targets of such racism—whites had long held black Africans in equal contempt—but many early white Americans had a particular loathing for Indians. A typical expression of that blind hatred was an 1850 editorial in a Kansas newspaper. It called Indians "a set of miserable, dirty, lousy, blanketed, thieving, lying, sneaking, murdering, graceless, faithless, gut-eating skunks as the Lord ever permitted to infect the earth."[2]

White settlers did not, however, push Indians off their lands and take over those domains simply out of arrogance and racism. Out-and-out greed was another defining feature of the removal policy. To the whites, land was precious not only as living space but also as property with monetary value. As more and more Europeans moved to America, they could not resist the temptation to satisfy their desire for land by seizing territory that had long been occupied by Indians. Moreover, white leaders often provided legal means for such seizures, while shredding former treaties that had promised the lands in question would always belong to the Indians.

Who Scalped Whom?

Still another defining trait of Indian removal was the brutality with which it was frequently carried out. A common stereotype perpetuated over the centuries depicted Indians as warlike, violent, and particularly savage in their treatment of whites when at war with them. Native American warriors were in fact often fearsome and efficient killers in wartime. But in most cases they went to war with whites only when provoked by white abuses. Also, white brutality in such conflicts commonly matched and quite often exceeded that of the Indians.

Scalping is a clear example. The gruesome practice has long been closely associated with Native Americans. But in reality, writes James Axtell, a historian at Virginia's College of William and Mary, it is likely that more Indian scalps were taken by early American settlers and frontiersmen than white scalps were taken by Indians. Axtell arrived at this conclusion after conducting an in-depth study of scalping in colonial America. He stated, "If white Americans have assumed that only 'savage' Indians scalped, they are clearly misinformed. If [those whites] thought that scalping was particularly 'savage,' they conveniently turned a blind eye to their ancestors' adoption and encouragement of the practice and to far more heinous acts and practices in America's military past."[3]

One reason that early white settlers collected so many Indian scalps is that colonial authorities frequently paid handsome bounties for them. One New Hampshire woman, Hannah Dustin, was particularly adept at the practice. The inscription on a statue of her that still stands in her hometown says she slew ten sleeping Indian women and children and then quite efficiently scalped them.

In addition, at times taking scalps was a tactic in white efforts to wipe out entire Indian tribes. In 1755, for example, Spencer Phips, commander of the Massachusetts Bay Colony militia, issued a proc-lamation that called for the annihilation of the local Penobscot tribe. Colonists, he said, should "embrace all opportunities of pursuing, cap-turing, killing and destroying all and every one of the aforesaid Indi-ans." He then began listing bounties for Indian scalps, including those of children: "For every scalp of such [a] female Indian or [a] male In-dian under the age of twelve years, that shall be brought in as evidence of their being killed as aforesaid, [I will pay] twenty pounds."[4]

Death on an Enormous Scale

The list of Indian removal's defining characteristics is not complete without including the suffering of those removed, an onslaught of tor-ment and death inflicted on an enormous scale. Modern experts are not sure how many Native Americans inhabited the lands lying north of Mexico in 1500, before European settlement began. Estimates range from as low as 2 million to as high as 18 million. What is certain is that by the year 1900, only about 250,000 Indians were left in the United States. The vast majority of these shocking population losses were due to four factors—deaths in wars with whites, out-and-out murder by whites, succumbing to diseases introduced by whites, and the damag-ing effects of removing and relocating entire tribes.

During removal, Indians regularly died of starvation, exposure, ill-ness, and murder by the soldiers in charge of the forced marches. After the marchers had been relocated, starvation and illness continued to take a toll, as did deaths in new military conflicts with whites. In ex-amining these losses, Lenore A. Stiffarm and Phil Lane Jr. are among a number of modern scholars who view the overall destructive effects of the removal of more than one hundred Indian tribes as an example of genocide, the systematic eradication of an entire race or culture. "There can be no more monumental example of sustained genocide," they write, "certainly none involving a 'race' of people as broad and complex as this, anywhere in the annals of human history."[5]

A final defining feature of Indian removal was that its awful effects proved long lasting. Well into the twentieth century, several decades after the last major tribal removals, Indians had to deal with problems generated by those events. These problems included grinding poverty, neglect, land disputes, joblessness, and racial prejudice, among others. Over time, the situation slowly but steadily improved, although for many of the dispossessed tribes the recovery process is still ongoing. Considering the many destructive characteristics of Indian removal, it is no wonder that the late distinguished historian of the American West, Arrell M. Gibson, ranked that ruthless uprooting of entire peoples "among the tragedies of the ages."[6]

Chapter 1

What Conditions Led to Native American Relocation?

T he large-scale, legal, and well-organized removal of Indian tribes from the eastern United States in the early 1800s marked an important watershed in relations between white Americans and Native Americans. Indians had been forced from their ancestral lands many times before. But not until the creation of a formal policy for removal by the US Congress in 1830 did this controversial practice become so orderly and efficient, and so sweeping in its scope.

The conditions leading up to the government's formal adoption of Indian removal policy were not new or the result of any sudden or revolutionary events. Rather, those conditions had evolved in a twisting, tortuous path over the course of more than two centuries. During those years, relations between Native Americans and the Europeans who colonized what is now the United States steadily deteriorated. In 1829 farsighted historian Jared Sparks wrote that the upcoming removal of the eastern tribes "only defers the fate of the Indians." He predicted that "in half a century, their condition beyond the Mississippi will be just what it is now on this side. Their extinction is inevitable."[7]

One Potential Impediment

Non-Indians first began to settle the region that would later become the United States in the early 1600s. English colonists arrived on the coasts of Virginia and Massachusetts, and the French and other Europeans were not far behind. Only one potential major impediment stood in the way of the settlers' expansion inland: The splendid countryside that stretched before them was already inhabited by people that the Italian explorer Christopher Columbus had more than a century before dubbed *Indians*. (The term derived from his initial assumption that he had reached the Indian Ocean.)

It became immediately apparent to the European newcomers that the natives were very different from them. The Indians had no formal territories or countries with set boundaries, for example. Neither did they have large-scale cities, architecture, road systems, or other aspects of culture that the Europeans associated with civilization. The natives also lacked guns and large sailing ships armed with cannons. Their skin was darker than that of most Europeans, and they knew nothing of Christianity, Europe's prevailing religious faith. These facts convinced the white settlers that the Indians were racially and culturally inferior to themselves.

Yet at first the Europeans refrained from trying to exploit that supposed inferiority, mainly because they needed the Indians' help. For example, in 1607 several hundred English settlers founded a colony at Jamestown, on the shore of Chesapeake Bay in Virginia. The first winter they experienced was harsh, but fortunately for them the local Indians took pity on them and gave them food and other supplies. At least for a while, therefore, the colonists and Indians coexisted in peace. A similar situation prevailed in the English settlement established at Plymouth, Massachusetts, in 1609.

Basic Differences over Land Use

It did not take long for the relations between the settlers and local natives to sour, however. White populations steadily grew, prompting the settlers first to ask for, then to demand, and finally to forcefully take

English settlers arrive at Chesapeake Bay, where they founded the Jamestown colony in 1607. The settlers survived the first harsh winter with help from local Indians.

nearby parcels of land from the Indians. As might be expected, the latter felt threatened, and hostilities between the two groups ensued. In fact, although over time whites and Indians had many disputes and quarrels, those over land ownership and exploitation were usually the most basic and divisive.

At the very core of this mutual disagreement was the simple fact that each side viewed land and how it should used quite differently. White Europeans had a tradition of personal land ownership stretching back untold numbers of centuries. They held that a person bought, inherited, or was given a piece of land that was marked off by specific boundaries. It belonged to that person alone, until the owner decided to sell it, give it away, or pass it on to heirs. Furthermore, in a case in which ownership of a newfound piece of land was in dispute, the party that first invested in developing it—by farming it, for instance—became the owner.

In contrast, to most Indians the idea of people owning land was alien. They believed that God (whom they commonly called the Great Spirit) had given the forests, plains, mountains, lakes, and so forth to all people to use when and as needed. Many Native Americans relied on the land for hunting and fishing, their chief means of obtaining food. Because game was sometimes more plentiful in one area than another, hunting Indians periodically moved their villages from place to place within a given region.

In contrast, a number of tribes, especially in the eastern sector of what would become the United States, obtained most of their food from farming. Typically, they raised maize (a kind of corn), squash, beans, and pumpkins. Sometimes they supplemented their vegetables with meat they acquired either by hunting or trade with hunting tribes. Farming Indians only rarely moved their villages, and when they did it was to seek out richer soil after the ground they had been using for a generation or two had become depleted of nutrients.

Like Wild Beasts?

Wherever Indians lived or moved to, the lands they inhabited had no artificial boundaries, as white-occupied lands did. "The country was made without lines of demarcation," stated Chief Joseph, the renowned leader of the Nez Percé tribe, "and it is no man's business to divide it." Similarly, people had no right to buy and sell land like the white Europeans did. "The one who has the right to dispose of it," said Chief Joseph, "is the one who has created it."[8]

White settlers typically regarded this idea of universal lands existing for the collective use of any and all people as primitive and hopelessly naive. Furthermore, their strong belief in their own natural superiority informed them that their concept of land use and ownership was the correct one and the Native American version was wrong. Therefore, the whites had every right to take possession of the lands stretching inward from the Atlantic coast.

Indians Spiritually Inferior?

Starkly different views of land use and ownership were not the only conflicting cultural aspects that separated white settlers and Native Americans and contributed to white feelings that Indians were inferior. Religion was also an area of frequent dispute and controversy. Almost all the settlers were Christians who believed in a single, all-powerful god. In contrast, native religious beliefs and rituals varied from place to place, although most Indian belief systems had some general ideas in common.

One such concept was that nature is filled with a kind of spiritual power or authority, often translated into English as the Great Spirit. Also, individual elements of that power inhabit animals, plants, lakes, mountains, and other facets of the natural world. Indians believed that they and their personal lives were connected with these spiritual elements in mysterious ways.

White Christians viewed these native beliefs as wrongheaded and held that their own faith was the only true one. As a Boston missionary arrogantly told Red Jacket, chief of northern New York's Seneca tribe, "There is but one religion, and but one way to serve God." He continued, "you have never worshipped the Great Spirit in a manner acceptable to him, but have, all your lives, been in great errors and darkness." This notion—that non-Christian Indians were spiritually inferior to white Christians—was repeatedly cited as a reason the two races could not live together, thereby justifying the removal and relocation of native tribes.

Quoted in William L. Stone, *The Life and Times of Sa-go-ye-wat-ha, or Red Jacket*. Whitefish, MT: Kessinger, 2010, p. 273.

A number of early settlers produced written arguments to bolster the white rationale for seizing Indian lands. Among the earliest was Jamestown preacher Robert Gray, who said in 1609, "These savages have no particular property in any part or parcel of that country, but only a general residence there, as wild beasts have in the forest." As would be the case with a rabbit or bear in the forest, therefore, "if the whole land should be taken from them [the Indians], there is not a man that can complain of any particular wrong done unto them."[9]

Later a petition created by settlers in Alabama used a similar excuse for taking Native American lands. The Indians, the document argued, "have by estimation nearly 100,000 acres of land to each man." Even worse, the settlers said, the natives did not build towns and farms on the land, but instead simply roamed around hunting for food, "like so many wolves or bears."[10]

Justifying Land Seizures

In the eyes of most whites, these and similar arguments supported their continued confiscation of Indian lands in the decades that followed European arrival. Some whites also justified such seizures by pointing out that the natives were savages. What made them savage, in this view, was that they were non-Christians who worshipped false gods or evil spirits, inferior in intelligence, lacking in morals, and bloodthirsty by nature.

In contrast, the settlers' rationale continued, whites were inherently benevolent and peaceful. They were also inherently smart, hardworking, and both God-fearing and favored by God. So in their view, it was only natural and inevitable that as they valiantly fought to tame a hostile wilderness, inferior species—including animals and Indians—should and would be displaced.

During and well beyond America's colonial period (1607–1776), these periodic dislocations of native tribes did not follow any master plan, but rather were carried out on a random, informal basis. For the Indians involved, however, there was no difference between these removals and the ones that would be carried out by formalized government decree in a later era. In both cases tribes were driven from their ancestral lands and forced to try to survive and recover their dignity either in strange, hostile surroundings or in small reservation-like compounds where their movements were highly restricted.

Indians as Obstacles

One of the first known examples of this destructive scenario was the series of events that followed the 1607 founding of Jamestown in Virginia, a region then inhabited by the Powhatans. (They are sometimes also called the Algonquians because they spoke dialects of the Algonquian language.) Although the natives initially befriended the settlers when the colony was established, many of those Indians came to regret it.

The initial reason for that change of heart revolved around the tobacco plant. In 1610–1611 one of the settlers, John Rolfe, started experimenting with growing tobacco from seeds obtained from the Powhatans. The first substantial shipment of Rolfe's crop reached England in 1614, creating a sensation that in turn fueled a large demand for Virginia-grown tobacco.

That situation marked a pivotal turning point both in Jamestown's existence and in relations between the settlers and natives of Virginia and nearby regions. Responding to the rapidly expanding tobacco market in Europe, the colonists swiftly put more acres of local land into production for the crop. When every available square foot of arable ground in the original colony had been planted, colonists eagerly began chopping down the nearby forests, in which the Powhatans had hunted for generations.

This series of events eventually put the English settlers on a collision course with the natives. The two peoples maintained a shaky peace for a few years, thanks mainly to the efforts of the leading Powhatan chief, Wahunsenacawh. He was willing to refrain from violence if the colonists stopped taking over the Indians' hunting grounds. But his hopes were in vain. The colony kept growing, and after he died in 1618 his brother, Opechancanough, became chief and decided that force was required to halt white expansion.

Whites Are like Serpents

Tecumseh, whose name meant "shooting star," wanted to halt the ongoing removal of Native Americans from their traditional hunting grounds. To that end, he spent several years attempting to unite the remaining eastern Indian tribes into an anti-white alliance. Historians think that, like modern politicians, he repeatedly used a few standardized speeches, altering them slightly to fit his audiences' regional cultural differences. This was likely the case with the speech excerpted here, which he delivered to the Creeks, Chickasaws, and Choctaws of the US Southeast.

> Brothers: When the white men first set foot on our grounds, they were hungry. They had no place on which to spread their blankets, or to kindle their fires. They were feeble. They could do nothing for themselves. Our fathers sympathized with their distress, and shared freely with them whatever the Great Spirit had given his red children. They gave them food when hungry, medicine when sick, spread skins for them to sleep on, and gave them ground so that they might hunt and raise corn. Brothers: The white people are like poisonous serpents. When chilled, they are feeble and harmless, but invigorate them with warmth, and they sting their benefactors to death.

Quoted in Bruce E. Johansen and Donald A. Grinde Jr., *The Encyclopedia of Native American Biography*. New York: Henry Holt, 1997, pp. 385–86.

All-out war erupted in 1622 when Powhatan warriors assaulted several of Jamestown's outlying villages, killing 350 residents. In response, the colonists began slaughtering the Indians on a mass scale. Year after year whites launched attacks on Powhatan settlements, butchering every man, woman, and child. After more than two decades of conflict, only around one thousand of the local Indians, who had numbered roughly twenty times as many in 1607, remained. The colonists removed them from their remaining lands and herded them onto a tiny sliver of territory in King William County in eastern Virginia. Though not called an Indian reservation at the time, for all intents and purposes it was one of the first.

Another of the many Indian peoples removed from their traditional lands by whites in America's colonial period were the Meskwaki, more familiarly known as the Fox. The tribe initially inhabited the Great Lakes region, especially the area along the southern rim of Lake Superior. In the mid- to late 1600s, the Fox came into contact with French trappers and settlers, who saw the natives as a barrier to their own expansion.

The result was a series of wars fought between the Fox and French between 1701 and 1742. During these years, the tribe's numbers dropped from about sixty-five hundred to between five hundred and one thousand. In desperation, the survivors allied themselves with the Sac (or Sauk) people, whose language and culture were very similar. In the end, however, constant pressure from the French, and some British settlers too, forced the Fox, along with the Sac, to migrate southward into Iowa and Illinois.

A New White Nation

In the years following the displacement of the Sac and Fox, the French, British, and other European colonists continued to show a perpetual thirst for new lands to settle and exploit. So war, or else the threat of either war or extermination, forced more and more native tribes off their ancestral lands. White civilization's westward march was briefly interrupted, however, by a war fought between the British colonists and their mother country.

That conflict was the American Revolution, which started in 1776. The colonists fought mainly over principles such as freedom, equality, and the rights to self-determination and the pursuit of happiness. The new white nation that emerged from the fray—the United States—had a unique opportunity. It could have reversed the destructive trends established by European colonial Indian policy by extending the same principles the colonists had fought for to Native Americans.

This did not occur, however, in part because distrust and hatred between the two sides were by now too deeply ingrained. Also, the revolution against Britain had done nothing to alter white feelings that Indians were inferior beings. As a result, Arrell M. Gibson pointed out:

> Leaders of those Indian tribes who lived astride the expansion path of the infant United States quickly learned that the new nation's leaders showed little originality in their approach to dealing with them, their lands, and other resources. Rather, they copied techniques used by European nations, particularly those developed by Great Britain. The ideals of human rights for all people expressed in the Declaration of Independence, the Preamble to the Constitution, and the Bill of Rights had yet to be extended to Indians.[11]

Fraudulent Dealings

One thing that did change when the United States formed was that there were no longer several competing white policies—one British, one French, and so forth—for dealing with native tribes. The US president and Congress now had charge of formulating a single approach to dealing with Indians. The new nation prided itself on being a country run by laws. So it was important to maintain the impression that the government obtained Indian lands in a lawful, aboveboard manner.

The chief legal device in this respect was the Indian treaty. Between 1778 and 1868, the country negotiated 374 treaties with various Native American peoples. As a result of these agreements, numerous tribes allowed whites to settle on lands formerly occupied solely by Indians. The problem was that despite the pretense of legality represented by these documents, many were purposely designed to mislead the natives.

Powhatan's warriors massacre Jamestown settlers in 1622. The colonists responded by slaughtering Indians on a mass scale.

The real intention was to take away the Indians' control of the lands and/or to remove the Indians from them altogether. To this end, treaties frequently featured deceptive language or technical fine print that Indians lacked the expertise to decipher.

Due to such tactics, some Native Americans who negotiated treaties believed those documents merely allowed whites to hunt on or travel across the domains in question. Only later did the Indians learn they had signed away most or all ownership rights. A leader of the Oglala Sioux was one such misinformed treaty signer. The white negotiators "came out and brought papers," he later recalled. "We could not read them, and they did not tell us truly what was in them."[12] Black Hawk, a chief of the Sac tribe, had a similar experience. "I touched the goose quill to the treaty," he complained, "not knowing, however, that by that act I consented to give away my village."[13]

The outcome of such fraudulent dealings is well illustrated by the very first Indian treaty signed by the United States, negotiated with the Delawares in 1778. American leaders wanted the tribe to aid them in their ongoing war against the British. In return, the treaty promised, when the war was over the Delawares would be eligible to join other Indian tribes in the Ohio Valley "to form a state whereof the Delaware nation shall be the head, and have a representation in Congress."[14]

Giving the Delawares and other tribes their own state in the new nation seemed to the Indians a deal too good to pass up. Unfortunately for them, it was actually a deal too good to be true. The white negotiators slipped in a loophole stating that the deal would go forward "provided nothing contained in this article [is] to be considered as conclusive until it meets with the approbation [approval] of Congress."[15] The Indians were told that congressional approval was merely a formality that would almost certainly happen. They did not realize that no one in the national legislature had any intention of approving such a deal. Sure enough, over the years this and other treaties the Delawares signed allowed the government to remove them from their lands. Members of the tribe ended up in Canada, Oklahoma, and other distant locations.

Jefferson on Indian Destiny

A few American leaders were embarrassed by such shady dealings. The third US president, Thomas Jefferson, for instance, said that they brought "dishonor to the American character." After the government had in effect driven a number of natives from their homelands, "they cannot love us,"[16] he stated. Perhaps, he added, future treaties with the Indians might be negotiated in a more just manner.

Yet even the innately fair-minded Jefferson could not guarantee that the periodic removal and relocation of Native American tribes would cease any time soon. Like other US leaders, he knew how most white Americans felt about the country's future. There was a growing belief that it was their destiny to continue moving into and absorbing the vast stretches of fertile territory lying west of the Appalachian Mountains. The now familiar term for that westward expansion, *manifest destiny*, would not be coined until much later, in 1845. But the concept itself—that the relentless growth of the United States was fated and inevitable—had already taken firm root by the time of Jefferson's presidency.

Jefferson himself felt that such expansion would be essential to the country's growth and future prosperity. In his view, these developments would be driven by the efforts of tens of thousands of hardworking small farmers who would settle in and tame the wilderness. As for the Indians already inhabiting that wilderness, they would have two basic choices, he suggested. Either they would themselves become small farmers and steadily accept and blend into white society, or they would need to move elsewhere, presumably to the little-known regions lying west of the Mississippi. Jefferson was one of the many whites who naively assumed that Indians could live by hunting and fishing almost anywhere. He also did not consider that the tribes who already dwelled west of the Mississippi might see Indians migrating from the East as intruders.

Tecumseh on Indian Destiny

Jefferson's native contemporary, the renowned Shawnee chief Tecumseh, had a very different vision of Native Americans' future. Born in 1768 in the Ohio Valley, as a young man he witnessed almost constant strife between Indians and whites. After Ohio came under US control in the 1790s, many of his people moved westward into what are now Indiana and Missouri.

Having experienced what was in effect removal from his forebears' ancestral lands, Tecumseh became determined to ensure that Indians would not experience such an outrage again. There was only one way to accomplish this hugely challenging goal, he realized. It was to unify most, and preferably all, of the remaining eastern tribes against continuing white expansion. Over the course of months and years, Tecumseh traveled widely, using his great gift for oratory in an attempt to rally his fellow Native Americans. In one now famous speech, he asked:

Where today are the Pequot? Where are the Narragansett, the Mohican, the Pocanet, and other powerful tribes of our people? They have vanished before the avarice and oppression of the white man, as snow before the summer sun. Will we let ourselves be destroyed in our turn, without an effort worthy of our race? Shall we, without a struggle, give up our homes, our lands, bequeathed to us by the Great Spirit? The graves of our dead and everything that is dear and sacred to us? I know you will say with me: Never! Never![17]

The struggle against the whites that Tecumseh spoke of did not necessarily have to be a violent one, he pointed out. In fact, he hoped that bloodshed could be spared on both sides by employing a new approach to diplomacy. In a nutshell, no single tribe would sign any treaty with the United States dealing with land ownership. The land "belongs to all," Tecumseh insisted. "No tribe has the right to sell it, even to each other, much less to strangers."[18] So all future treaties would be negotiated by representatives of all the tribes, who would present a united front that would force the whites to deal fairly with the Indians.

This grand dream of Native American unity did not come to pass, however. To his credit, Tecumseh did manage to bring together several Indian peoples in a common effort against white encroachment. But a pan-Indian alliance of the great size and degree of organization that was needed never quite came together in a timely way.

Nonetheless, the resolute Tecumseh doggedly fought on to the bitter end. Hoping it would help his cause, he allied himself with the British against US forces in the War of 1812, and he died in battle in October 1813. One of his last known statements to his fellow Indians urged them to do whatever was necessary to hold tight to the lands that had sustained them and their ancestors. "Our lives are in the hands of the Great Spirit," he declared. "We are determined to defend our lands, and if it be his will, we wish to leave our bones upon them."[19]

The problem was that no other Native American leader carried on Tecumseh's work in a meaningful way after his death. Also, white leaders saw the lost cause of Indian unity as an opening to put more pressure than ever on individual tribes to vacate their lands. Indian removal was about to evolve from an episodic, haphazard occurrence into a calculated, organized policy fated to heap misery on one people and shame on another.

Chapter 2

Formulating Removal and Relocation Policy

In 1820, seven years after Tecumseh met his untimely end and ten years before the passage of the Indian Removal Act, about 120,000 Native Americans lived in the eastern United States. Often called the East for short, it was the extensive region stretching from the Atlantic Seaboard westward to the Mississippi River. That figure of 120,000 represented perhaps one-tenth, or possibly closer to one-twentieth, the number of Indians who had inhabited the East when Europeans started arriving in North America in the late 1400s and early 1500s. Exact figures are unknown. But modern population expert Russell Thornton estimates that in 1492 some 5 million Indians lived in what would become the United States, so the East likely contained at least 1.2 million and maybe as many as 2 million or more.

Those Indians who remained in the East in 1820 dwelled for the most part peacefully and quietly in a few small, scattered areas, primarily in the Southeast. Their little communities were surrounded on all sides by roughly 8.1 million white Americans and about 1.5 million black slaves. So the Native Americans accounted for a mere one-eightieth of the region's total population. It is uncertain how the slaves felt about that tiny minority of Indians in their midst. What is certain, however, is that most whites viewed even that extremely small number of Indians as too many.

One reason for this hostile attitude was a lingering fear of Indians among many whites. At some future time, the argument went, one of the tribes might rise up and murder its white neighbors, a notion clearly based on the stereotype of the savage Indian. Even some of the whites who knew that the scattered, long-since defeated Native Americans posed no real threat wanted them gone. First, Indian culture seemed too alien to that of white Americans, making the latter uncomfortable. Also, most whites assumed that the remaining tribes were still in the way of continuing white settlement of the East's wilderness areas. For these reasons, sentiment in favor of purging the East of Indians steadily grew among whites.

Could Indians and Whites Coexist?

The idea that white civilization would inevitably occupy and control all the lands east of the Mississippi was far from new in 1820. As far back as 1762, well before the British colonies broke away from their mother country, the noted inventor, politician, and future US founding father Benjamin Franklin remarked that all the territory lying east of the Mississippi "will in another century be filled with British people."[20]

Franklin's statement was unclear in regard to the fate of Native Americans, so some who read those words wondered how such American expansion would affect the Indians who had inhabited these lands for untold generations. Did Franklin think they could coexist with the "British people" who would eventually "fill" the eastern United States? As it turned out, in later words and deeds Franklin showed he was one of the few American leaders and thinkers who did believe the two peoples could reside together without fighting. Franklin biographer Carl Van Doren points out that he

> sympathized with the Indians. It was not they who broke treaties or drove greedy bargains or presumed on superior strength. He believed, with [fellow Pennsylvania leader] William Penn that civilized justice and savage justice were much the same and [that the two races] could live side by side in peace. What was needed was equitable agreements between the two races and honest trading.[21]

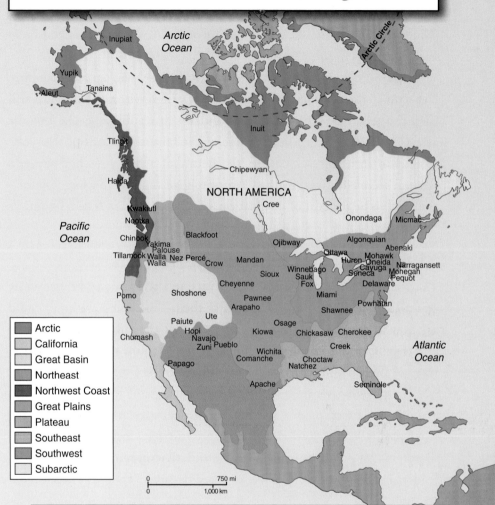

Native American Cultural Regions

Inupiat

Arctic Ocean

Arctic Circle

Yupik

Tanaina

Aleut

Tlingit

Inuit

Chipewyan

Haida

NORTH AMERICA

Cree

Pacific Ocean

Kwakiutl

Nootka

Chinook

Onondaga

Micmac

Blackfoot

Algonquian

Yakima

Palouse

Ojibway

Abenaki

Tillamook

Walla Walla

Nez Percé

Crow

Mandan

Ottawa

Huron

Mohawk

Oneida

Narragansett

Sioux

Winnebago

Sauk

Cayuga

Seneca

Mohegan

Pequot

Cheyenne

Fox

Pomo

Shoshone

Pawnee

Miami

Delaware

Arapaho

Powhatan

Paiute

Ute

Osage

Shawnee

Chumash

Hopi

Navajo

Kiowa

Chickasaw

Cherokee

Zuni

Pueblo

Wichita

Creek

Atlantic Ocean

Papago

Comanche

Choctaw

Natchez

Apache

Seminole

	Arctic
	California
	Great Basin
	Northeast
	Northwest Coast
	Great Plains
	Plateau
	Southeast
	Southwest
	Subarctic

0   750 mi
0   1,000 km

This map shows the major Native American cultural regions in North America as they were when the Europeans first arrived. It also names some of the tribes living in each region.

As time went on, however, most American leaders, along with a majority of the nation's citizens, disagreed that white-Indian coexistence was possible. They took a much more aggressive stance. Typical by 1820 were the views of future president William Henry Harrison, who had led the US forces that had defeated and killed Tecumseh in 1813. Not long before that pivotal battle, Harrison had conceded that a great many Indians had already been removed from the East. But those who remained there, he said, lived on some of the choicest and most valuable lands in the region.

This did not sit well with Harrison and those who agreed with him. "The most fertile tracts that are within our territorial lands are still their property," he grumbled about Indians in a public speech. Then he asked in an indignant tone, "Is one of the fairest portions of the globe to remain in a state of nature, the haunt of a few wretched savages, when it seems destined by the Creator to give support to a large population and to be the seat of civilization, of science, and of true religion?"[22]

The Case for Removal: Jefferson

The answer to this pointed question was, in the opinion of most white Americans, a resounding no. Also, if those "wretched savages" could not stay in the East, it logically followed that they must go somewhere else. Furthermore, most whites held, if the Indians would not agree to leave of their own accord, they would have to be forcibly removed.

The growing sentiment for ridding the East of its remaining Indians was not based on any particular political speech or writing by any single white leader. Rather, the case for creating a formal, legislated Indian removal policy was made in a cumulative manner by several white leaders over the course of close to three decades. Thomas Jefferson led the way.

In April 1803, during his first term as president, his administration bought an enormous piece of land—the Louisiana Territory—from France. Louisiana, as most people came to call it, stretched from what is now Montana in the Northwest to what is now the state of Louisiana in the South. Covering more than 800,000 square miles (2.1 million sq. km), it contained portions of fourteen future US states, overall nearly doubling the size of the country.

In Jefferson's view, this sudden windfall, almost all of it lying beyond the Mississippi, gave the nation more than huge amounts of

Cherokee Literacy

One reason the Cherokees felt they should be allowed to continue living among whites was that they had recently made a major effort to become literate, using a new system that recorded their own language on paper. Devised by a Cherokee named Sequoyah, the system used eighty-six symbols borrowed from various ancient alphabets, each symbol standing for a sound in the Cherokee language. Scholar A.J. Langguth tells how Sequoyah convinced his skeptical fellow tribe members that he had succeeded. First, he brought together six neighbors and asked each to deliver a speech.

> As a man spoke, Sequoyah made marks on tree bark with pokeberry juice. When the man finished, Sequoyah read back to him what he had just said. Hearing their words repeated accurately amazed and convinced them. Sequoyah drew up a chart, with one character for the sound of "s," which could be combined with other syllables. He found that a Cherokee could learn his symbols in only one week. After that, to form words simply meant arranging them in the order of their sounds. He taught the system to his six-year-old daughter, and a group of her friends. Taking the children to a Cherokee National Council meeting, he asked them to transcribe messages that he dictated to them separately. Then he collected the results, shuffled them, and passed them out to different children. When they read them back perfectly, the dazzled council adopted Sequoyah's [system] for use by the entire Cherokee nation.

A.J. Langguth, *Andrew Jackson and the Trail of Tears to the Civil War*. New York: Simon and Schuster, 2010, pp. 69–70.

priceless natural resources. It also seemed to provide a way to solve the ongoing Indian problem. He and his advisors reasoned that a portion of Louisiana could be set aside as a new home for those eastern Native Americans who could not assimilate into white society. In the same year that the deal with France occurred, Jefferson predicted to Harrison that over time the Indians in the East would "either incorporate with us as citizens of the United States, or remove beyond the Mississippi."[23]

The Case for Removal: Monroe

In addition to Jefferson's remarks, the acquisition of Louisiana set in motion other intermittent discussions, speeches, and writings about the fate of the eastern tribes. Over time, these made establishing a formalized Indian removal policy increasingly attractive to white Americans. President James Monroe forcefully contributed to the ongoing debate in 1825, near the end of his second term. By that time, he and most other US leaders had concluded that Harrison had been right to assert that Indians and whites could not coexist. Referring to the natives, Monroe stated:

> Experience has clearly demonstrated that in their present state it is impossible to incorporate them in such masses, in any form whatever, into our system. It has also demonstrated with equal certainty that without a timely anticipation of and provision against the dangers to which they are exposed, under causes which it will be difficult, if not impossible, to control, their degradation and extermination will be inevitable.[24]

Monroe's suggestion that the eastern Indians were in danger and therefore must be protected was a roundabout way of pointing out a grim reality—that any significant resistance by Indians to US policy and white society would likely result in the natives' extinction. It was therefore only a matter of common sense, Monroe said, that the Indians accept the supposedly generous US offer of relocation and protection. In his words, "To prevent intrusions on their property, to teach them by regular instruction the arts of civilized life, and to make them a civilized people—is an object of very high importance. It is the powerful consideration which we have to offer to these tribes as an inducement to relinquish the lands on which they now reside and to remove to those which are designated."[25]

Indian Territory

The exact location of the lands "which are designated," as Monroe put it, was unclear, even to him. As Jefferson and others had proposed several years earlier, the eastern Indians would almost certainly end up somewhere west of the Mississippi. But the domains lying beyond that great river were nothing less than immense. At the time that Monroe left office, no one had yet determined precisely where in that vast expanse the native tribes would be relocated.

In the eight to nine years that followed, US politicians and government policy makers steadily came to agree on the exact boundaries of the area in question. They also gave it a name—Indian Territory (or Indian Country). Finally formalized by Congress in the 1834 Indian Intercourse Act, it initially encompassed most of the region now covered by the states of Oklahoma, Kansas, Nebraska, Iowa, the Dakotas, and Montana.

In this way the case for creating a formal Indian removal policy was made over the course of more than a generation. Yet none of the presidents who led the country in those years seriously considered implementing a major round of actual Indian removal. This included Jefferson, his immediate successor James Madison, Monroe, and Monroe's successor John Quincy Adams. In part this was because during their terms, a number of eastern tribes actually moved away on their own, although reluctantly. During Jefferson's tenure, for instance, most of the Sac and Fox migrated to Illinois, Iowa, and Missouri, and by 1820 some of the Choctaws had left Mississippi and entered what is now Oklahoma. It is also likely that none of these presidents had any desire to preside over the tremendous strife that was bound to occur when tens of thousands of people were forcibly driven from their homes.

"The Most Aggressive Enemy"

It was Adams's successor, Andrew Jackson, who instigated that strife by implementing an official Indian removal policy. A major military figure, Jackson had been acclaimed as a national hero for his victories over the British during the War of 1812. He had also made a name for himself as a longtime adversary of Indians. After defeating the Creek Indians in 1814, for example, he helped negotiate the treaty that stripped them of 22 million acres (8.9 million ha) of their lands in Georgia and Alabama.

Jackson apparently did not harbor any overt hatred of Indians. He even called himself their friend on a number of occasions. Yet there is no doubt that he accepted that era's common racist views of them. That is, the natives were foul savages who were inferior to whites, and the two races were better off living far apart. That made Jackson, as scholar Peter Farb says, "utterly insensitive to the treatment of the Indians,"[26] and it explains why he avidly pushed for the passage of major Indian removal legislation. For these reasons, the late American historian Howard Zinn called Jackson "the most aggressive enemy of the Indians in early American history."[27]

For their part the Indians were both bewildered and frustrated that most whites were so intolerant of the Native Americans living among them. A Creek chief named Speckled Snake expressed how much the Great Father, the title many Indians used to describe the sitting US president, had disappointed him. "I have listened to a great many talks from our Great Father," he said in 1829 about Jackson's recent speeches. "But they always began and ended in this—'Get a little farther; you are too near me.'"[28]

Heated Debates Begin

Speckled Snake made those remarks a few months into Jackson's first presidential term. At the time, more than one hundred thousand Indians still lived in the East, among them members of the Cherokee, Chickasaw, Choctaw, Creek, and Seminole tribes. For anyone who was not yet sure how the new president felt about these peoples and their fate, Jackson included some hints in his inaugural address. "It will be my sincere and constant desire," he stated, "to observe toward the Indian tribes within our limits a just and liberal policy, and to give that

US and French officials take part in a ceremony marking the formal transfer of land under the Louisiana Purchase. The purchase nearly doubled the size of the United States.

humane and considerate attention to their rights and their wants which is consistent with the habits of our government."[29]

On the surface this statement sounded positive and sincere, and some white Americans assumed it meant the new president intended to treat the Cherokees and other eastern tribes fairly. But a closer reading of the passage revealed his true intentions. The Indians' rights and wants, he said, would be dealt with in a manner "consistent with the habits" of the government. The past habits of the US government had been to drive Indians from their lands and to violate the terms of treaties made with them—so present-day Indians could expect the new president to dish out more of the same.

True to form, Jackson did not take long to turn his attention to the eviction of the Cherokees and other tribes living in Georgia. The campaign to expel Native Americans from that state began with the creation of the Indian Removal Act, which Congress formally began debating early in 1830. The essence of the bill was that it would give the president the authority to select any tribe living on US-controlled lands and relocate it to new lands lying beyond the Mississippi River.

The congressional and public debates leading to the bill's passage were heated. The legislators who opposed the act pointed out that the Cherokees in Georgia had largely given up their old tribal ways. They had built white-style houses and farms, adopted white-style clothing, and become literate, so they had earned the right to be treated the same way as white Georgians.

In contrast, the bill's supporters, who were in the majority, argued that these so-called cultural improvements did not matter. Deep down, the Cherokees were still Indians, who were, by their nature, inferior to white folk. Those making this argument laced their speeches with overt written and verbal attacks on Indians in general and the Cherokees in particular. One such attack came from one of the president's close associates, Lewis Cass, governor of the Michigan Territory and soon to become Jackson's secretary of war. In a statement in the January 1830 issue of the *North American Review*, Cass said in regard to Indians in general, "It is difficult to conceive that any branch of the human family can be any less provident [wise] in arrangement, less frugal in enjoyment, less industrious in acquiring [wealth], more implacable in their resentments, more ungovernable [unruly] in their passions, with fewer principles to guide them." More specifically about the Cherokees, Cass claimed he could not find "upon the face of the globe a more wretched race."[30]

Jackson's Ultimatum

Such vicious character assassinations helped push the Removal Act through Congress and onto Jackson's desk. He signed it into law on May 28, 1830. In the close to four years that followed, he and other US leaders, including several in Georgia's local government, put increasing pressure on the Cherokees to pack up and leave the state on their own. Otherwise, those officials warned, sooner or later the government would have to send in the army and remove them by force.

"You Will Ultimately Disappear"

I n May 1835 President Andrew Jackson issued an ultimatum explaining why the Cherokees living in Georgia must vacate their homes and lands and resettle in Indian Territory. "My Friends: I have long viewed your condition with great interest," he began. He had known the Cherokees during periods of both peace and war, which was why he felt sincere concern for their current situation. Jackson continued:

> You are now subject to the same laws which govern the other citizens of Georgia and Alabama. You are liable to prosecutions for offenses, and to civil nations for a breach of any of your contracts. Most of your young people are uneducated, and are liable to be brought into collision at all times with their white neighbors. Your young men are acquiring habits of intoxication [drunkenness]. With strong passions, and without those habits of restraint which our laws inculcate [instill] and render necessary, they are frequently driven to excesses which must eventually terminate in their ruin. The [wild] game has disappeared among you and you must depend upon agriculture and the mechanical arts for support. And yet, a large portion of your people have acquired little or no property in the soil itself, or in any article of personal property which can be useful to them. How, under these circumstances, can you live in the country you now occupy? Your condition must become worse and worse, and you will ultimately disappear, as so many tribes have done before you.

Quoted in John Ehle, *Trail of Tears: The Rise and Fall of the Cherokee Nation.* New York: Doubleday, 1988, pp. 275–76.

In the meantime, though in the minority, some white Americans were appalled at both the widespread anti-Indian racism and the mounting threats against the Cherokees and other tribes. Sickened by the removal idea, a US representative from New York, Henry Storrs, publicly denounced it. Recalling early colonial times, he said, "We came to these people with peace offerings and they gave us lands."[31] Yet, he pointed out, the colonists had repaid that kindness by turning on the Indians. Storrs resolutely proclaimed that he would not take part in turning on them again.

Such statements of support for the Cherokees and other Native Americans did not deter Jackson from his mission to rid the East of Indians. Seeing that the many warnings he had given the Georgia-based Cherokees had failed to budge them, he decided to take a more forceful approach. On April 7, 1835, he issued them an ultimatum, saying that they should start preparing to leave their homes. Although he began the message with the sociable salutation "My friends," Jackson repeatedly spoke to the Cherokees as if they were children. He also insulted them by indirectly but plainly calling them uncivilized. It was no longer possible for them to "flourish in the midst of a civilized community,"[32] he stated.

"You have but one remedy within your reach," Jackson went on. "And that is to remove to the West." Moreover, "the sooner you do this, the sooner you will commence your career of improvement and prosperity." There was but one choice for the Cherokees, the president cautioned. "The fate of your women and children, the fate of your people to the remotest generation, depend upon this issue."[33]

The president's speech did not specifically mention the use of force. But his message was clear. Any Indians who refused to leave would find themselves without government protection and completely at the mercy of both their white neighbors and the US Army. This frightened some Cherokees enough that they began preparing to move. The majority of the tribe's members, however, boldly decided they would continue to resist. They were unable to imagine the barefaced display of cruelty and brutality to which they were about to be subjected, part of which former president John Quincy Adams would later call "an eternal disgrace upon the country."[34]

Chapter 3

Uprooting and Relocation

The news of President Andrew Jackson's demand that the Georgia Cherokees pack up and leave their homes sent waves of distress and alarm through their community. Tribal leader John Ross was shocked and angry as well as distressed. He had personally known the president for decades, having fought, along with other Cherokees, on his side against the British in the War of 1812. He was stunned that Jackson had gone so far as to threaten to evict the tribe from its lands.

It was not the first time, however, that the president had disappointed the leading Cherokee chief. Back in January 1831, a few months after the Indian Removal Act had become law, Ross had expressed his frustration in a letter to a white friend no less famous than Jackson. This was legendary frontiersman Davy Crockett, then a US representative from Tennessee. How the president could so cruelly "withdraw from us the protection pledged by treaty, and to allow the state of Georgia to usurp from us the rights and liberties of freemen," Ross wrote, "I cannot understand."[35]

Still, for a long time Ross had believed that Jackson had pushed for the Removal Act mainly to intimidate some eastern tribes into moving away on their own. As long as the Cherokees held fast and refused to move, Ross reasoned, they would prevail and retain their lands. Thus, he did not anticipate that the president would actually use force to remove the tribe. As A.J. Langguth describes it, Ross simply "could not believe that the government of the United States would forcibly dispossess fifteen thousand of the continent's original owners."[36]

A Separate Accord

Following the April 1835 ultimatum, however, it was clear to Ross that he must find some new way to negotiate with the government. There had to be a strategy he could use, he thought, that would appease Jackson and his supporters while at the same time ensuring that the tribe could stay on its ancestral lands. Perhaps, as Ross would later tell some Florida Indians, a courageous people threatened with removal could throw themselves "upon the generosity and justice of the American people."[37]

Regrettably for Ross, his frantic attempts to find a solution to the pressing dilemma were seriously complicated by major divisions within the tribe. He led the larger of two factions—the so-called National Party. Representing about thirteen thousand to fourteen thousand of the roughly fifteen thousand to sixteen thousand Georgia Cherokees, its members wanted to keep resisting US removal policy. The other group, numbering roughly two thousand tribal members, was led by John Ridge and his father, known as Major Ridge. They advocated giving in and accepting the government's demands to relocate to the West.

To that end, the Ridges approached US officials separately and negotiated an accord called the Treaty of New Echota. It specified that the Cherokees would sell their land in the East, consisting of some 8 million acres (3.2 million ha), to the government in return for the sum of $5 million, and then migrate to Indian Territory. Not long before the scheduled signing ceremony in late December 1835, Major Ridge solemnly addressed a large group of his followers. Speaking of the graves of the Cherokees' ancestors, he said, "I would willingly die to preserve them, but any forcible effort to keep them will cost us our lands, our lives, and the lives of our children. There is but one path of safety, one road to future existence as a nation. That path is open before you. Make a treaty of cession [surrender]. Give up these lands and go over beyond the great Father of Waters [the Mississippi]."[38]

Meanwhile, Ross and other leaders of the National Party strenuously objected to the treaty. It did not represent the wishes of the vast majority of Georgia Cherokees, they argued. Ross assumed that this fact would be enough to make the government back off from signing the document. But he was wrong. Although they knew better, Jackson and a majority of the members of the Senate, which ratifies treaties, acted as if the agreement did represent all the Cherokees. The Senate ratified the treaty in March 1836, and the Ridges and their approximately two thousand followers departed Georgia for the West the following year.

"No Cry, No Sob Was Heard"

In the meantime, while they awaited the government's next move, Ross and his supporters continued to discuss their own upcoming strategy. Although they did not want to lose their homes, they worried about the consequences of their continued refusal to leave. In particular, they agonized over what might happen to Cherokee women and children. They had heard the horror stories about other eastern tribes that had received government demands to vacate their lands in recent years. Even those tribes that had agreed to head westward on their own had suffered enormously while migrating.

The grim experience of the Choctaws of Mississippi was a case in point. In the late 1820s their white neighbors had tried to get them to move away by almost ceaselessly making their lives miserable. Among the many illegal and/or inhumane tactics employed were stealing or killing the Indians' livestock and pilfering or destroying their crops. The Indians found that complaining to the white authorities was useless, since both local and state officials were complicit in the harassment.

By 1830 the Choctaws could take no more. They grudgingly decided to migrate, and late in the following year some thirteen thousand members of the tribe packed up and headed west. The trip proved horrendous for numerous reasons. Viewing a large group of Indians on the move as a potential threat to the safety of white Americans along the proposed route, the government sent soldiers to escort the marchers.

These troops turned out to be more than mere guards, however. Like slave drivers, many of them cruelly drove the Choctaws through mud, sleet, snow, and freezing temperatures. Little by little, struggling over steep hills and through putrid swamps, the Indians inched their way westward. Many died along the way.

The corn harvest gets underway in a Choctaw village. The Choctaws of Mississippi gave in to the cruel harassment of their white neighbors and agreed to migrate to Indian Territory. Thousands died along the way.

At the time, Alexis de Tocqueville, a twenty-five-year-old Frenchman, was visiting Tennessee. He saw some soldiers herding a large number of Choctaws onto a riverboat, part of their reluctant journey westward. "I was the witness of sufferings which I have not the power to portray," the young man wrote. He went on:

It was then the middle of winter, and the cold was unusually severe. The snow had frozen hard upon the ground, and the river was drifting huge masses of ice. The Indians had their families with them, and they brought in their train [rear section] the wounded and sick, with children newly born, and old men upon the verge of death. They possessed neither tents nor wagons, but only their arms and some provisions. I saw them embark to pass the mighty river, and never will that solemn spectacle fade from my remembrance. No cry, no sob was heard amongst the assembled crowd. All were silent.[39]

Based on both the testimony of witnesses and later estimates by experts, roughly twenty-six hundred, or about one-fifth, of the Choctaws died on their way to Indian Territory. Besides disease and exposure to the cold, another common cause of death was starvation. Some eyewitnesses said that young children went as long as six days with nothing to eat, and many elderly folk went much longer, until some fell along the roadway, never to get back up. Others lost their lives to cholera, an intestinal infection brought on by drinking water contaminated by deadly bacteria. Although government authorities had been quick to surround the marchers with guards, no one had thought to send along a single doctor.

The Fate of the Creeks

As hard a time as the Choctaw migrants had, at least they had made the decision to journey westward on their own. Those who resisted removal and were forced to leave suffered even more. The Creeks of Tennessee, Georgia, and Alabama, for instance, had long resisted white demands to migrate, but they had steadily lost ground in the literal as well as figurative sense. The Creek contingent that Jackson had defeated in Alabama in 1814 had handed over large stretches of Creek lands to the US government. Other land cessions to the whites had followed in 1818 and 1821. The chief of one group of Creeks, William McIntosh, warned that the rest of its holdings were at risk and that there was a real

The aged Major Ridge, who with his son headed the minority Cherokee faction that opposed the National Party, addressed his supporters shortly before signing the Treaty of New Echota. The elder Ridge said in part:

> I am one of the native sons of these wild woods. I have hunted the deer and turkey here, more than fifty years. I have fought your battles, have defended your truth and honesty, and fair trading. The Georgians have shown a grasping spirit lately; they have extended their laws, to which we are unaccustomed, which harass our braves and make the children suffer and cry. I know the Indians have an older title than theirs. We obtained the land from the living God above. They got their title from the British. Yet they are strong and we are weak. We are few, they are many. We cannot remain here in safety and comfort. I know we love the graves of our fathers. We can never forget these homes, but an unbending, iron necessity tells us we must leave them.

Quoted in Thurman Wilkins, *Cherokee Tragedy: The Story of the Ridge Family and the Decimation of a People.* New York: Macmillan, 1970, pp. 276–77.

chance "the little band of our people, poor and depressed, will be left to wander without homes and be beaten like dogs."[40]

The potential that this dismal prophecy might come true seemed to increase when another group of Creeks traded away their lands in the East to the government in 1826. As they departed for the West, federal officials began pressuring the remaining Creeks to do the same. Meanwhile, as Arrell M. Gibson told it, land-hungry settlers assisted the officials by carrying on a merci-less campaign of harassment. Squatting on Creek lands, stealing Indian livestock, and tormenting the Creeks until they fought back, they created incidents that were characterized as savage Indian reprisals. Like Georgia and Mississippi, the Alabama legislature abolished the Creek tribal government and made all Indians subject to state law, which did not protect Indians from white aggression but did protect whites from Indian retaliation. By 1832, the Creek chiefs were finally persuaded of the futility of attempting to live in the land of their ancestors.[41]

In the four years that followed, white soldiers rounded up most of the remaining Creeks and herded them into camps in Alabama. In the process, the Indians were forced to abandon their homes and almost all of their belongings. Then, during the bitterly cold winter of 1836–1837, the army marched close to fifteen thousand of them to Indian Territory. Some thirty-five hundred members of the tribe, including virtually every infant and most of the elderly, died along the way.

The Seminole Resistance

The Georgia Cherokees who awaited their own fate during the fol-lowing winter and spring also recalled the struggles of another Indian people that had recently resisted removal. That tribe, the Seminoles, had long dwelled primarily in northern Florida. They had steadfastly resisted removal until 1832, when some of them decided it would be better to leave rather than risk the tribe's destruction. They signed a treaty with the federal government that gave them three years to put their affairs in order and begin migrating. The agreement promised that the tribe would get $15,400 for its Florida lands and $3,000 a year while its members settled into their new lands beyond the Mississippi.

However, a small faction of Seminoles refused to leave. Led by Chief Osceola, they staged a rebellion in which more than one hundred white soldiers died in 1835 alone. Osceola threatened that he and his warriors would fight "till the last drop of Seminole blood had moistened the dust

Seminole chief Osceola awaits his fate after being arrested by US authorities who lured him to a meeting for peace talks that were never intended to take place. Osceola was later imprisoned in South Carolina.

of my hunting ground."[42] Unable to defeat Osceola and his followers, the US military general who had been given that task, Thomas Jesup, resorted to treachery. In October 1837 Jesup called for peace talks, and Osceola went to him under a flag of truce. Instead of honoring it, the general seized the chief and sent him in shackles to a prison in South Carolina.

At the time of Osceola's arrest, Georgia Cherokee chief John Ross was warily awaiting the government's next move against his own tribe. A month later, Ross was surprised by a sudden request from the administration of the new president, Jackson's successor Martin Van Buren. Van Buren's secretary of war, Joel R. Poinsett, knew that Ross was an effective leader and negotiator who had a good reputation among other Indians. So Poinsett asked Ross to talk with some of Osceola's followers who were still resisting Jesup. Poinsett offered the Cherokee leader a deal that was hard to refuse. If Ross succeeded in talking those remaining Seminole rebels into working with Jesup rather than fighting him, it would make the Cherokees' own upcoming negotiations with the government go smoother.

With a bit of newfound hope, Ross hurried to Florida. There he sought out and met with the rebels and told them, "I know that a brave people, when driven to a state of desperation, would sooner die under the strong arm of power than to shrink and die the death of a coward. But I will speak to you as a friend, and with the voice of reason advise you, as a small but brave people, to act the part of a noble race."[43]

The noble thing to do now, Ross advised the Seminoles, was to save the tribe from further death and grief. If they agreed to meet with Jesup, they might work out some kind of arrangement beneficial to all involved. The Indians accepted Ross's argument and went under a white flag to speak with Jesup. But just as he had done to Osceola, the general dishonorably broke the truce, arrested them, and threw them in jail. Dazed and mortified, Ross pleaded with the Seminoles to believe that he had not purposely betrayed them. Rather, he insisted, the general had deceived him as much as he had them.

Time Runs Out

The disgruntled Ross wasted no time in traveling to Washington, DC, to complain to Poinsett about Jesup's duplicity. But when the war secretary began making excuses for Jesup, it became clear that Poinsett had only been using the Cherokee chief to further the government's position. Ross now realized there were few white leaders he could trust to do what he believed was the right thing for his people.

Ross also wrestled with the fear that despite all his hard work trying to reverse the government's removal plans, he may have done his people a disservice. As late as the early months of 1838, most of them still clung to the hope that his tireless efforts on their behalf would somehow pay off in the end. Therefore, few of them had prepared for a major move. In fact, in historian Brian Hicks's words, "most Cherokees went about their business as if there were no shadow over their land." Instead of preparing for the inevitable, "many were actively planting gardens for the summer crop."[44]

Like Swine to Market

Christian missionary Daniel S. Butrick, who spent some twenty years working among the Georgia Cherokees, witnessed the overland march that came to be called the Trail of Tears. His long, riveting account includes this passage describing how the soldiers put the Indians in grave danger when loading them into riverboats in Arkansas. "Forcing them into filthy boats, to overflowing," he said, was

only a most expensive and painful way of putting the poor people to death. The first company sent down the river, including those dear trembling doves who spent a night at our house, were, it appears, literally crammed into the boat. There was, we understand, a flat bottom boat, 100 feet long, 20 feet wide, and two stories high, fastened to an old steamboat. This was so filled that the timbers began to crack and give way, and the boat itself was on the point of sinking. Some of the poor inmates were of course taken out, while this boat was lashed to the steamboat, and some other small boats were brought to take in those who had been recalled [unloaded]. Twelve hundred, it is said, were hurried off in this manner at one time. Who would think of crowding men, women, and children, sick and well, into a boat together with little, if any more room or accommodations than would be allowed to swine taken to market?

Quoted in Vicki Rozema, ed., *Voices from the Trail of Tears*. Winston-Salem, NC: Blair, 2003, p. 141.

But time finally ran out for the Georgia Cherokees. On April 6, 1838, the War Department ordered General Winfield Scott to take charge of a force of soldiers and ensure that the Indians complied with the removal order. By early May, Scott had gathered some twenty-two hundred federal troops. He also took charge of members of the Georgia state militia and volunteers from nearby North Carolina, Tennessee, and Alabama. That brought his forces to a strength of more than seven thousand.

Arriving in the region where most of the Cherokees lived, Scott met with several local chiefs and told them their people must be ready to leave their homes within a few weeks. First, they would stay for a short period in holding camps protected by stockade fences. Then, when all tribal members had assembled, they would begin the trek toward their new homes in the West. Scott also placed an announcement in the state's newspapers to make sure that all Cherokees were aware of what they must do.

The Trail of Tears

On May 17 the general addressed his soldiers and in forceful terms said he expected them to execute the removal as humanely and mercifully as possible. A decent individual, Scott sincerely meant it. But many of the troops, perhaps out of disdain for Indians, did not follow these orders. When the actual removal began on May 26, there was widespread abuse of Cherokees by soldiers, as well as disgraceful, unlawful behavior by many of the Indians' white neighbors. According to a detailed study conducted by nineteenth-century anthropologist James Mooney:

> Families at dinner were startled by the sudden gleam of bayonets in the doorway and rose up to be driven with blows and oaths [swear words] along the weary miles of trail that led to the stockade. Men were seized in their fields or going along the road, women were taken from their [spinning] wheels and children from their play. In many cases, in turning for one last look as they crossed the ridge, they saw their homes in flames, fired by the lawless [white] rabble that followed on the heels of the soldiers to loot and pillage.[45]

The Cherokee people face hunger, disease, and death along the Trail of Tears. Thousands died in the forced march to their new homes in the West.

These crimes and injustices, which went unpunished, marked only the beginning of the horrors the Cherokees faced during the removal process. After Scott's men had collected thousands of tribal members in the holding camps, the actual westward march, which came to be called the Trail of Tears, began. White Christian missionary Daniel S. Butrick, who had worked among the Cherokees for twenty years, witnessed the removal up close. From the Indians' "first arrest," he later wrote, "they were obliged to live very much like brute animals, and during their travels were obliged at night to lie down on the naked ground, in the open air, exposed to wind and rain, and herd together, men, women, and children, like droves of hogs, and in this way, many were hastening to a premature grave."[46]

Numerous other white witnesses told similar stories. A Maine resident traveling in the South saw part of the Cherokee migration and penned an account of it. Printed in January 1839 in the *New York*

Observer, it said in part, "Even aged females, apparently nearly ready to drop into the grave, were traveling with heavy burdens attached to the back, on the sometimes frozen ground, and sometimes muddy streets, with no covering for the feet except what nature had given them." The witness added that the soldiers buried fourteen or fifteen Indians "at every stopping place."[47]

Even some of the soldiers who carried out the removal were appalled by the operation they had been forced to take part in. One of them was Colonel Z.A. Miles, a member of Georgia's state militia. "I fought through the Civil War and have seen men shot to pieces and slaughtered by the thousands," he later wrote. "But the Cherokee removal was the cruelest work I ever knew."[48]

A Pall of Darkness

The devastated, bedraggled band of Cherokees reached the far side of the Mississippi early in 1839. Of the roughly fourteen thousand of their number who had departed Georgia the year before, more than four thousand had died along the trail. The survivors, meanwhile, were exhausted, hungry, and broken in spirit.

Yet this massive infliction of human misery was only a single component of a larger tragedy—the devastation of the eastern tribes. By the early 1840s Indian removal in the East was nearly finished. At that point more than sixty thousand Native Americans had been uprooted from their traditional lands, but not all of them had made it to Indian Territory. Some fifteen thousand, or a quarter of them, had perished along the way.

Speaking specifically about the Cherokees' suffering, in December 1838 the missionary Butrick called their recent ordeal "a year of spiritual darkness."[49] At that moment in time, neither he nor the tens of thousands of Native Americans who had been transplanted to Indian Territory realized that their troubles were far from over. An even larger pall of darkness and misery was about to descend upon them.

Chapter 4

Problems and Suffering of the Relocated Tribes

B y the mid-1840s, most members of the Indian tribes that had once occupied sections of the eastern United States had relocated to the large expanse lying beyond the Mississippi River. Among those tribes were not only the handful of more populous peoples like the Cherokees, Choctaws, Creeks, and Seminoles, but also many dozens of smaller groups, including the Apalachees, Biloxis, Catawbas, Corees, Hattaras, Mattaponis, Nanticokes, Pamunkeys, Saponis, and Tuscaroras, to name only a few.

Some tribes or factions of them had, under pressure by white neighbors and the government, migrated on their own. Others, like most of the Georgia Cherokees, had been brutally removed from their lands and driven to the places allotted to them in the West. The question now was whether the majority of relocated Indians would be able to prosper and build a future in their new homes. Some believed the government's negotiators when they assured them that the removal treaties they had signed would protect them and allow them to thrive for generations to come.

Others who had been displaced did not believe these promises. After all, they reasoned, white leaders had lied to and cheated Native Americans countless times before. Why should anyone believe them now? As it turned out, those Indians who were wary of the guarantees made in the treaties were right to be suspicious. In most cases the relocated tribes did not prosper in Indian Territory, but rather faced a host of problems that wreaked havoc on them no less than the removal had.

Seeing the Bigger Picture

Not all of the US negotiators who persuaded the eastern Indians to move had knowingly and purposely lied to them. Some of the agents, especially those not in top leadership circles, had been sincere. They had believed that, in spite of the negative effects of the removal process, the government would do the right thing and keep its promises to the relocated peoples.

In contrast, a number of the higher-placed officials, even the well-meaning ones, were less sure that those promises would be kept. By the 1830s and 1840s, it was becoming increasingly clear to those who could see the bigger picture of ongoing US expansion that it was not likely to stop at the Mississippi River. The concept of manifest destiny was quietly but steadily taking hold of the imaginations of politicians, big businessmen, financial planners, and others whose principal interest was US economic and territorial growth. They sensed that relocating the eastern Indians would likely prove only a stopgap measure and that those tribes would probably face further upheavals.

Most of the white Americans who foresaw those upheavals believed that they were necessary to the country's growth and the happiness of its people. Andrew Jackson had stated that necessity in a nutshell in December 1830, asking, "What good man would prefer a country covered with forests and ranged by a few thousand savages to our extensive Republic, studded with cities, towns, and prosperous farms," a land "filled with all the blessings of liberty, civilization, and religion?"[50]

The opposite, pro-Indian view, held by an extreme minority of white leaders and intellectuals, was summarized later, in 1844, by the noted painter and writer George Catlin. The term *manifest destiny* had not yet been coined, so he called the nation's relentless westward march the "blasting," or exploding, frontier. "From the first settlements of our Atlantic coast to the present day," he said, "the bane of this blasting frontier has regularly crowded upon them [the Indians], from the northern

Relocation Under the Indian Removal Act of 1830

WISCONSIN TERRITORY

MICHIGAN

NEW YORK

UNORGANIZED TERRITORY

IOWA TERRITORY

SAUK

1832

FOX

PENNSYLVANIA

Mississippi R.

Arkansas R.

ILLINOIS

INDIANA

OHIO

Ohio R.

MISSOURI

Mississippi R.

Trail of Tears

KENTUCKY

VIRGINIA

INDIAN LANDS

TENNESSEE

NORTH CAROLINA

ARKANSAS

New Echota

TEXAS REPUBLIC (1837–1845)

CHICKASAW 1832

CHEROKEE 1835

SOUTH CAROLINA

CHOCTAW 1830

CREEK 1832

GEORGIA

Rio Grande

MISSISSIPPI

ALABAMA

Atlantic Ocean

LOUISIANA

FLORIDA TERRITORY

1832

SEMINOLE

Gulf of Mexico

→ Routes taken by Indians
☐ Land ceded by Indians, with date of cession
☐ Land ceded to Indians

to the southern extremities of our country; and, like the fire in a prairie, which destroys everything where it passes, it has blasted and sunk them and all but their names into oblivion, wherever it has traveled."[51]

Outright Lies

In the meantime the public as a whole was not nearly as farsighted about the Indians' ultimate fate. Most white Americans knew that a number of tribes had recently been removed and relocated, mainly through reading intermittent newspaper reports. But very few were aware of exactly how the dire deed had been accomplished. Indeed, the vast majority of US citizens had no idea that this large-scale roundup of Indians had come at a cost of unimaginable cruelty, misery, and death.

Instead, most Americans believed the statements issued by government agents and spokesmen, which were purposely designed to mislead and pacify the general public. Typical was one by Commissioner of Indian Affairs Thomas H. Crawford. Not long after the Cherokees had been relocated, he boldly lied about it, saying, "Good feeling has been preserved, and we have quietly and gently transported [thousands of our Indian] friends to the west bank of the Mississippi."[52]

Martin Van Buren also lied outright in his December 3, 1838, State of the Union Address, delivered even while the brutal Trail of Tears episode was unfolding. The removal process, he said, had "had the happiest effects." Moreover, the Indians' westward journey "has been principally under the conduct of their own chiefs, and they have emigrated without any apparent reluctance." After making several more mainly untrue statements in the speech, the president claimed that his government's dealings with the tribes "have been just and friendly throughout. Its efforts for their civilization [have been] constant and directed by the best feelings of humanity. Its watchfulness in protecting them from individual frauds [has been] unremitting."[53]

Viewed as Intruders

In retrospect, the purpose of these lies is clear. Crawford, Van Buren, and other US leaders knew that most white Americans viewed the majority of Indians as inferiors. Yet those officials feared that if the general public knew the extreme level of cruelty and brutality used to enforce Indian removal, there might be a backlash of sympathy for the displaced natives.

This policy of keeping the bulk of the population in the dark about the treatment of the relocated tribes continued well after the natives reached Indian Territory. If the relocation process had been a resounding success, no cover-up would have been necessary and the government would likely have allowed the Indians to speak for themselves about their newfound happiness. After all, that would have made Jackson,

A Permanent Home?

Like Andrew Jackson before him, Martin Van Buren assured the Indians who had been relocated, Congress, and the American people that the US government was well meaning. Once the eastern tribes had been relocated west of the Mississippi, he said, the land would be theirs forever. No whites would intrude and disturb the Indians' lives and prosperity. Van Buren made these promises in his December 3, 1838, State of the Union Address, stating in part:

> The recent emigrants [to Indian Country], although they have in some instances removed reluctantly, have readily acquiesced in [agreed to] their unavoidable destiny. They have found at once a recompense [reward] for past sufferings and an incentive to industrious habits in the abundance and comforts around them. There is reason to believe that all these tribes are friendly in their feelings toward the United States; and it is to be hoped that the acquisition of individual wealth, the pursuits of agriculture, and habits of industry will gradually subdue their warlike propensities and incline them to maintain peace among themselves. To effect this desirable object the attention of Congress is solicited to the measures recommended by the Secretary of War for their future government and protection, as well from each other as from the hostility of the warlike tribes around them and the intrusions of the whites. The policy of the government has given them a permanent home and guaranteed to them its peaceful and undisturbed possession.

Quoted in Collected State of the Union Addresses of U.S. Presidents, "Martin Van Buren, December 3, 1838." www.infoplease.com.

Van Buren, and other architects of Indian removal seem like brilliant statesmen and great humanitarians. However, forced relocation turned out to be mostly disastrous, so the cover-up continued.

One major reason for the abject failure of the removal and relocation program was that many of the lands to which eastern tribes were shipped were already occupied by western tribes. Often Indians from one part of the continent had noticeably different cultures than those in other regions. In some cases they managed to bridge their differences and maintain mutual peace. But frequently, compelling them to live in close proximity proved a formula for misunderstanding, suspicion, and even violence.

Such clashes between competing tribes in Indian Territory began even before the major Indian removals of the 1830s. In 1808 and 1809, for example, a small group of Cherokees left their homes in South Carolina. For their own reasons and of their own accord, they moved to the Arkansas Territory, part of the larger area that would soon be called Indian Territory. A few years later, in 1817, the US government recognized this band of people as the Kituwahs, or "western Cherokees."

The problem was that the Arkansas region to which these Cherokees migrated was already inhabited by the Osage Indians, who viewed the newcomers as intruders. Over time, the two peoples raided each other's villages, stealing livestock and causing other sorts of mischief. In 1817 a western Cherokee revealed only a tiny slice of the ongoing conflict when he contacted a US territorial official, complaining, "We wish you to pity us, for the Osages are deaf to all we can say or do. They have stolen two of our best horses and killed two of our young men."[54] The hostilities came to a head later that year in a large battle fought near present-day Claremore, Oklahoma, in which more than eighty Osages perished. The Cherokees eventually drove the remaining Osages into what is now Kansas.

Similar conflicts among Native American groups in Indian Territory occurred in the decades that followed. One of the many tribes involved was the Pawnee, which had originally inhabited what is now eastern Nebraska. Along with the Otos, Iowas, Omahas, and others, they were among the so-called Border Indians, who dwelled along the eastern margins of the Great Plains. As white society pushed various eastern tribes across the Mississippi, those displaced peoples put increasing pressure on the Pawnees and other Border Indians. In turn, the Border Indians moved westward into the hunting grounds of the fierce Sioux, Cheyenne, and Arapahoe tribes. Arrell M. Gibson explained that "swift-riding warriors from these tribes regularly preyed on the Border Indians and the more westerly immigrant [relocated] Indians for livestock, women, and weapons. The constant threat of these forays discouraged the [immigrants from] beginning life anew in the western wilderness."[55]

Lurking Negative Forces

These wars among some of the native peoples in and near Indian Territory marked only the start of serious troubles that would come to affect both indigenous tribes and newcomers alike. A number of the relocated Indians thought they might avoid such strife, because they actually managed to prosper for a while after arriving from the East. The Georgia Cherokees, for instance, established farms, ranches, and towns. They also built schools and opened shops, newspapers, and other businesses.

But these positive, at times remarkable accomplishments were undercut by lurking negative forces that steadily gripped the region. Much of the trouble derived from the fact that several key east-to-west trails already crisscrossed Indian Territory. At first the two most important were the Oregon and Central Overland Trails. Traffic on these wilderness tracks—made up of frontiersmen, trappers, and a trickle of settlers—remained fairly light in the century's first decades. But it slowly increased over time.

Then in 1849 that flow of travelers on the trails exploded, thanks to the discovery of gold in California the year before. In the span of only five or six years, an estimated 150,000 people, most of them white, swarmed from the East Coast to California. Another revealing statistic shows that the non-Indian population of California was fourteen thousand early in 1848. A mere two years later it was close to half a million.

A majority of those making up this mighty human flood passed

Miners pan for gold in California. Thousands of gold seekers journeyed through Indian Territory en route to California, where they hoped to strike it rich.

through Indian Territory. Some of the local warriors felt they had a right to physically resist the intruders. But the more prudent chiefs decided it was better to try diplomacy first. In the late 1840s the leaders of one tribe complained directly to President James K. Polk, suggesting it was only fair that the whites crossing their lands pay them tolls. "We have all along treated the [trespassers] in the most friendly manner," the Indians told Polk, "giving them free passage through our hunting grounds." But there was a limit to their generosity, the petitioners declared. "We are poor and beg you to take our situation into consideration. It has been customary when our white friends make a road through the Red Man's country to [pay] them for the injury caused thereby."[56]

When the government ignored these requests, some tribes tried to collect such tolls on their own, which often led to enmity and even bloodshed between Indians and whites. Meanwhile, the white intruders established trading and military posts in Indian Territory. Some of these facilities remained staffed for many years to come and helped attract droves of white homesteaders, cattle ranchers, buffalo hunters, and railroad builders to the area.

The Civil War in Indian Territory

Far exceeding this disruption of the Indians' way of life in the region was what happened there after the outbreak of the American Civil War in 1861. In that enormously bloody conflict, the nation's Northern states opposed the Southern ones, which had seceded, or separated, from the Union. The Southern states formed their own country—the Confederate States of America, or Confederacy for short. The Confederates immediately saw a chance that many of the tribes that had recently left the South for Indian Territory might become their allies. The supposition was that these Indians would sympathize with the Confederacy rather than the Union.

Since the tribes in question were still at odds with the government in Washington, DC, that had so callously uprooted and displaced them, this theory proved largely correct. Several of the tribes dwelling in Indian Territory eagerly allied themselves with the Confederacy. They included the Creeks, Choctaws, Chickasaws, Seminoles, and Cherokees, the latter still led by Chief John Ross.

Meanwhile, Union leaders managed to persuade several other Native American groups to fight on their own side. Indians on both sides were organized into formal regiments, which opposed each other in numerous fierce battles. Some of those encounters were small. But others involved thousands of fighters and produced many casualties.

After much death and destruction, in late 1864 and early 1865 the Civil War was nearing an end. At that point, according to University of Tulsa scholar Garrick Bailey, who is of Cherokee and Choctaw heritage,

anarchy prevailed throughout most of Indian Territory. Union and Confederate deserters, Indians and non-Indians alike, formed outlaw gangs and roamed the countryside, indiscriminately killing, burning, and looting. In the last months of the war, some of the high-ranking Union officers joined in the lawlessness, stealing over three-hundred thousand head of Indian-owned cattle.[57]

"You Are Fools"

At the start of the Civil War, a handful of Indian leaders warned that Indians who sided with some whites against others were embarking on a fool's errand. One of these leaders was Dakota chief Little Crow. He scolded those Indians who thought the Civil War was an opportunity for Native Americans, saying:

> Yes, they [the whites] fight among themselves, away off. Do you hear the thunder of their big guns? No, it would take you two moons [months] to run down to where they are fighting, and all the way your path would be among white soldiers as thick as tamarack trees in the swamps of the Ojibways. Yes, [the whites] fight among themselves, but if you strike at them they will all turn on you and devour you and your women and little children, just as the locusts in their time fall on the trees and devour all the leaves in one day. You are fools. You cannot see the face of your chief. Your eyes are full of smoke. You cannot hear his voice. Your eyes are full of roaring waters. Braves, you are little children. You are fools. You will die like the rabbits when the hungry wolves hunt them.

Quoted in Famous American Trials, "Little Crow." http://law2.umkc.edu.

The results of these events were no less than catastrophic for all the residents of Indian Territory. Up to a quarter of the population of most of the tribes in the region died in the fighting, and thousands more were maimed for life. Moreover, the area's entire economy was devastated, as every barn, store, office, and public building was burned to the ground. Making matters even worse, after the Union won the war in 1865, the government proceeded to void all of the Indian treaties signed at the start of the conflict and seized large portions of Indian Territory.

Confident in Superior Numbers

At least a few of the Indian leaders who fought against either the Union or Confederacy during the Civil War foresaw that in the long run it did not matter which side won. One, a Dakota chief named Little Crow, correctly reasoned that sooner or later that victor would turn on its Indian allies. Referring to white people, he told his fellow Dakotas, "You may kill one, two, or ten, and ten times ten will come to kill

A Union officer meets with Native American chiefs at Fort Rice in Dakota Territory around the time of the Civil War. Union leaders convinced some Native Americans to fight on their side.

you. Count your fingers all day long, and white men with guns in their hands will come faster than you can count."[58]

Other chiefs predicted that history would continue to repeat itself. As had happened in the past, they said, innumerable white settlers would set their sights on the Indians' most fertile and valuable lands and take them for themselves. This warning proved well founded. From the late 1860s on, large numbers of whites entered Indian Territory each year, in effect breaking the treaties their government had made with the relocated tribes. These settlers were more brazen than earlier ones in appropriating Native American lands. In part this was because the whites had become confident in their superior numbers and the vast industrial base that gave them railroads, cannons, and other technical advantages. Kent State University historian Philip Weeks adds, "Americans did not take long in resolving to fashion new and better lives for themselves and their families in these lands, or businessmen to recognize the commercial opportunities inherent in this situation, or the national government to see advantages in securing the region for the United States."[59]

The enormous upsurge in white westward migration steadily destroyed the original US plan, which had sought to keep the races separate by shipping the eastern Indians to the region beyond the Mississippi. As the two races once more occupied the same areas, the federal government again felt compelled to intervene. The onslaught of Indian removal and relocation that had begun years before in the East now continued in the West, destroying and displacing tribe after tribe.

The Case of the Cheyenne

Among these devastated Native American peoples were the Cheyenne (or Cheyennes). When the United States formed in the 1770s, separate bands of their culture lived in the Black Hills of South Dakota, the Powder River region of Montana, and elsewhere in the Great Plains. When Indian removal caused widespread havoc in the plains in the 1870s, the Cheyenne resisted white intrusion, prompting the US Army to pursue them. Eventually, during the winter of 1876–1877, their leading chief, Dull Knife, was forced to surrender.

The defeated Cheyenne were at first shipped to a section of Indian Territory, which by that time had considerably shrunk from the acreage it had occupied when created in the 1820s and 1830s. Life for the tribe's members was extremely difficult, in part because the land assigned to them was barely farmable. Also, they were ravaged by diseases they had caught from white people.

Faced with these dilemmas, the Cheyenne, still led by Dull Knife, decided to escape. About three hundred of them headed north in September 1877, and soon afterward some ten thousand soldiers and three thousand white civilians gave chase. When the pursuers caught up, a skirmish occurred in which more than one hundred Cheyenne died. By the time the government placed the survivors on a small patch of land in Montana, only eighty of them were left. Like the dwindling members of numerous other tribes, they were about to experience the beginnings of the long and bitter legacy of US Indian removal.

Chapter 5

What Is the Legacy of Native American Removal?

The patch of land in Montana on which the last few Cheyenne ended up was an example of something that became increasingly common in the West in the 1860s and 1870s—the Indian reservation. The idea of confining Native American tribes to remote parcels of land was one of the principal legacies of Indian removal policy. The concept was based largely on a foregone conclusion—that the Indians' efforts to maintain their traditional way of life would sooner or later fail. After all the tribes had been defeated, white leaders reasoned, the survivors would have to live somewhere. Assigning them to reservations located well away from white population centers appeared to be the most logical solution to the problem.

The Harsh or Humane Approach?

Reservation-like areas where Indians dwelled on the fringes of white civilization had existed throughout the early 1800s and well before. But the formal policy of creating Indian reservations, frequently referred to as Concentration (meaning concentrating Indians in specific places), did not begin until the 1850s. In 1850 the commissioner of Indian Affairs, Luke Lea, stated that it was necessary that Indians "be placed in positions where they can be controlled, and finally compelled by stern necessity to resort to agricultural labor or starve."

About these "positions" where Native Americans should be placed, he said, "There should be assigned to each tribe, for a permanent home, a country adapted to agriculture, of limited extent and well-defined boundaries, within which all, with occasional exceptions, should be compelled constantly to remain until such time as their general improvement and good conduct may supersede [replace] the necessity of such restrictions."[60]

As time went on and the need for more reservations grew, some white leaders felt these land tracts should be, in effect, prison camps strictly monitored and controlled by the military. Indians living on them should be assigned mandatory menial work, and any who tried to escape should be shot on sight. An advocate of this harsh approach, noted army general Philip H. Sheridan, stated in June 1869 that all Indians "who do not immediately remove to their reservations, will be treated as hostile, wherever they may be found, and particularly if they are near [white] settlements or the great lines of communication."[61]

The chief advocate of a more humane approach to establishing reservations was former Civil War general and US president Ulysses S. Grant. Feeling the influence of the Quakers and other religious and humanitarian groups, in the early 1870s he adopted a series of policies that together came to be called Grant's Peace Policy. The object was to maintain harmony between Indians and whites by treating Native Americans with at least a modicum of dignity and respect, while still maintaining control over them.

First, Grant said, the reservations should be under the control of civilian officials in the Bureau of Indian Affairs, rather than the army. Further, the agents of the bureau should be nominated by the Quakers and other benevolent church groups. These agents would be tasked with protecting the tribes on the reservations from profiteers and other individuals seeking to cheat the Indians out of their lands and valuables.

Also according to Grant's plan, Indian agents sent by the bureau would provide the reservation Indians with an education and teach them how to become self-supporting farmers. Each reservation would be allotted, or subdivided, into individual farms or homesteads. The hope was that eventually—perhaps within a couple of generations—the

"Race Memory" of the Removals?

Although most of the eastern Cherokees were removed and marched to Indian Territory in 1838, a few of them remained behind. Of these, some hid in the mountains and eluded the soldiers who searched for them. A handful of others slipped away from Indian Territory and walked hundreds of miles back to the East. Altogether, these surviving eastern Cherokees numbered around one thousand in 1850. Today most of their descendants live on an 83-square-mile (215 sq. km) land trust called the Qualla Boundary, located in western North Carolina. The others live separately in towns and cities across the East.

In the 1990s one of the latter, Cynthia Kasee, a former professor at the University of South Florida, decided to travel for the first time to the area in Oklahoma where most of the relocated eastern Cherokees ended up back in the 1830s. Later she wrote about how she almost talked herself out of making the trip. "Why was I so apprehensive?" she asked in retrospect. "To understand the 'race memory' of the Indian removals, if you're not an Indian, try picturing yourself as a Jew visiting Auschwitz," the Nazi concentration camp where thousands of Jews were exterminated during World War II. Kasee continued, "I feared how overwhelming that race memory might be when I first stood as my ancestors had, looking into an Oklahoma night sky, remembering those who had not survived."

Quoted in Geary Hobson et al., eds., *The People Who Stayed: Southeastern Indian Writing After Removal*. Norman: University of Oklahoma Press, 2010, p. 180.

Native American farmers would abandon most of their former tribal allegiances and more or less blend into American society. It was this supposedly humane plan recommend by Grant, not the more militant one backed by Sheridan, that the government initially adopted to run the Indian reservations.

Continued Resistance

Though well meaning, however, Grant and other white leaders who agreed with him gave little or no thought to the plan's moral implications and the possible harm it might do to Indian peoples. In contrast, many Native American leaders did recognize the potentially destructive effects of the scheme. Their reactions often echoed what a Cherokee named Corn Tassel had said three decades before, during his people's removal. He told white leaders, "Many proposals have been made to us to adopt your laws, your religion, your manners, and your customs. But we confess that we do not yet see the propriety [correctness] or practicability of such a reform." Whites, he said, typically ask Indians why they do not farm like most whites. But could Indians not turn around and ask whites why they do not hunt for a living as Indians do? "The great God of Nature has placed us in different situations," Corn Tassel continued. "It is true that he has endowed you with many superior advantages. But he has not created us to be your slaves. *We are a separate people!*"[62]

Years later, in the post–Civil War era, many Indians still felt, as Corn Tassel had, that they should not be servants to white people. Even as the government began instituting Grant's new reservation policy, various tribes and bands of Indians continued to resist both white encroachment and forced assimilation. The Sioux (or Lakota) and some other Plains tribes, for example, openly opposed the US Army in the mid-1870s. This regional conflict climaxed in the Indians' annihilation of a cavalry force commanded by General George Armstrong Custer in 1876 in the Montana Territory.

Unfortunately for the Plains tribes, they were unable to follow up on that widely celebrated victory. First, they failed to maintain the unity and resolve that had made the victory possible. Second, white

General George Armstrong Custer charges into battle against thousands of Lakota Sioux and Northern Cheyenne Indians. Custer and more than 250 soldiers died.

society did not see the event as Indians everywhere did—as the brave act of a proud people desperately fighting to save their homes and way of life. Instead, whites typically viewed Custer's defeat as a monstrous massacre inflicted by wild, warlike savages. This only reinforced the belief that herding the Indians onto reservations where they could be controlled was an absolute necessity.

A More Desperate Approach

Thus, forced removal followed by relocation—no longer to large open regions but rather to smaller, confined reservations—continued in the

Luther Standing Bear's Contributions

Luther Standing Bear (1868–1939) made major contributions to reversing the terrible damages done to Native American culture by the US government's ill-advised removal and relocation policies. He was born in Rosebud, South Dakota, where his father, George Standing Bear, built and ran a small general store. George enrolled his son in the Carlisle Indian School in Carlisle, Pennsylvania, the country's first off-reservation school for Native American youth. Later, as a young man Luther Standing Bear joined Buffalo Bill Cody's famous Wild West show that toured the country and several foreign nations. Later still, Standing Bear traveled to California and made a name for himself as one of the leading Indian actors in Hollywood, with dozens of both silent and sound films to his credit.

A brilliant, thoughtful individual, he also wrote several books and articles aimed at educating white Americans about Indian culture. Some of these writings caught the attention of John Collier, who became commissioner of the Bureau of Indian Affairs in 1933. Standing Bear helped Collier and his advisers craft the enlightened Indian policies of President Franklin D. Roosevelt's administration. Two of Standing Bear's many keen observations of the differences between Indians and whites are: "Indian faith sought the harmony of man with his surroundings; the other sought the dominance of surroundings" and "For one man the world was full of beauty; for the other it was a place of sin and ugliness to be endured until he went to another world."

Luther Standing Bear, *Land of the Spotted Eagle*. Lincoln: University of Nebraska Press, 1978, pp. 196–97.

late 1870s and beyond. Some Indians valiantly persisted in resisting the tidal wave of white expansion they knew would engulf them in the end. The bold bid for freedom made in the winter of 1876–1877 by Dull Knife's band of Cheyenne is a memorable example.

A similar escape from a reservation occurred a few months later, in the summer of 1877. A few hundred Nez Percés led by Chief Joseph slipped out of their Idaho reservation and led thousands of soldiers on a daring 1,300-mile (2,092 km) chase. In October the courageous band made it to within a mere 30 miles (48 km) of the Canadian border and permanent freedom. But at the last moment the army caught up. To save the women and children, Joseph reluctantly surrendered, after which he uttered the now famous words, "I am tired. My heart is sick and sad. From where the sun now stands, I will fight no more forever."[63]

Joseph's surrender speech captured the sentiments of a certain number of the Indians who had been forced to languish on reservations. Their freedom of movement restrained and their lives tightly supervised by white soldiers and officials, they felt exhausted and overwhelmed. As Philip Weeks puts it, "they wrestled mightily with their new situation. Some actively sought to cooperate with the Americans. They believed that their accustomed way of life was gone forever and that their future depended on adaptation to their new role."[64]

Not all the remaining Indians felt this way, however, and some advocated continued resistance to white society's onrush. The question was how to go about it. A few, for instance, hid their children in an effort to evade the imposition of white-style education on their cultures. Others risked arrest by openly practicing certain traditional Native American religious rituals that the government had banned from the reservations.

Still other Indians seized on a more desperate approach. Known as the Ghost Dance, it was a mostly new religious belief that rapidly spread from one Plains reservation to another in 1890. Its proponents claimed its potent magic would save Native American civilization from doom by driving the entire white race eastward and into the Atlantic Ocean. Furthermore, wearing special shirts during worship would supposedly make Indians immune to white soldiers' bullets.

Fearing the Ghost Dance would inspire new Indian rebellions, US Army leaders ordered the so-called Ghost Dancers arrested. This policy culminated in a tragic episode in late December 1890. Hearing reports of a gathering of Sioux Ghost Dancers near Wounded Knee Creek in South Dakota, units of mounted army troops closed in. While the soldiers were making their arrests, a gunshot rang out. To this day, no one knows who fired it—an Indian or a soldier. Whoever it was, the shot pushed the jittery, trigger-happy troops into unleashing an enormous volley of bullets into a crowd of unarmed men, women, and children. In the space of a few seconds, 153 Indians were dead.

A New Round of Propaganda

The incident at Wounded Knee was the last major armed encounter involving Indians and the US military. At that point, around 250,000 Native Americans were left in the United States, perhaps one-twentieth as many as had inhabited the region before the Europeans arrived. Thanks largely to nearly three centuries of removal and relocation efforts, the surviving Indians had been thoroughly defeated, divided, and demoralized. In short, they had been rendered virtually harmless.

Yet the government wanted to go still further. Top officials decided to make sure that no Native Americans could ever again gain self-determination or any sort of political or economic power. The way to do that, they reasoned, was to keep the natives separated on their reservations. That would render them weak and dependent on the government for their most basic needs.

To sell this approach to the American people, who might at first glance view it as too harsh, it was vital for US leaders to make it appear that such steps were required for the Indians' own good. In this way, a new round of anti-Indian propaganda flowed from the Bureau of Indian Affairs and other government agencies. Not long after the Wounded Knee incident, a former commissioner of Indian Affairs, Hiram Price, issued public statements that repeated the standard stereotypes of Indians as less than civilized, dangerous people who were still "skillful in the use of the scalping knife." Only by living on the reservations where white Americans could patiently watch over, teach, and help them, he said, could the remaining Indians find "the pathway to civilization."[65]

Indeed, Price inaccurately asserted, US Indian policies were already showing some signs of progress. "The plow and sickle have, to a great extent, driven the tomahawk and the scalping knife from the field," he announced. "Thousands of Indians have learned that labor is ennobling and not degrading, and are beginning to see the dawn of a brighter future, when they may stand side by side with those whose aim is to make the world wiser and better."[66]

Such claims—that the government wanted only to better the Indians' lot—were belied by the realities of life on the reservations in the 1890s and well beyond. US officials restricted the Natives' freedom of movement, for example. An Indian could not leave the reservation or travel without a pass issued by a government agent, and obtaining such passes was difficult; it was not until 1924 that Indians were declared US citizens and permitted to travel at will. The government also denied them religious freedom, banning most traditional Indian rituals; kept them from governing themselves; and routinely turned a blind eye to the abject poverty that blighted large portions of the reservations. In addition, white officials frequently jailed Indians who protested that such rules and conditions were unfair and/or abusive.

Beginnings of Positive Change

Apart from the 1924 grant of citizenship, little changed on the reservations during the early decades of the twentieth century. Then in 1934 came the beginnings of some positive change in Indians' lives. Thanks to pressure from a few enlightened and progressive American leaders—notably President Franklin D. Roosevelt and his commissioner of Indian Affairs, John Collier—in that year Congress passed the Indian Reorganization Act, or Wheeler-Howard Act. It gave tribes the right to adopt their own governments on the reservations, set up tribal businesses to help improve local economic conditions, acquire government loans to build new schools and roads, and enjoy religious freedom.

In formulating these and other progressive policies, Collier was strongly influenced by a chief of the Oglala Sioux, Luther Standing Bear. Born in the nineteenth century in the midst of the final years of Indian removal, Standing Bear became one of the twentieth century's most prominent Native American authors, educators, and film actors. More than anyone else, he taught Collier and other white politicians how wrongheaded many former government Indian policies had been.

Standing Bear also tried to make white leaders understand how Native Americans viewed themselves, as well as whites, which helped bridge the cultural gap between the two peoples. One example of his wisdom begins, "The white man does not understand the Indian for the reason that he does not understand America. He is too far removed from its formative processes. The roots of the tree of his life have not yet grasped the rock and soil." In contrast, Standing Bear proclaimed, "in the Indian, the spirit of the land is still vested."[67]

Armed Native Americans show their anger at US Indian policy by taking control of the village of Wounded Knee in South Dakota in 1973. These and other protests forced the public and Congress to take note of long-standing grievances.

In addition to such observations of Indians, whites, and their relations, Standing Bear suggested some of the enlightened policies that Collier instituted. These policies did change some conditions on the reservations for the better. Many Indians felt they had taken some first steps toward independence, self-rule, and reasserting their identity as a people.

Nevertheless, numerous problems persisted. First, even after the improvements generated by the Indian Reorganization Act, poverty on most reservations remained entrenched and widespread. At the same time, although Indians could now leave their reservations whenever they desired, little of a positive nature awaited them on the outside. Anti-Indian racism was still rampant in much of the country; most banks would not grant Indians loans or mortgages; and good, well-paying jobs for Indians were close to nonexistent.

Activism Draws Public Attention

For these and other reasons, constructive change for Indians both on and off the reservations occurred very slowly in the years that followed. Starting in the late 1960s, however, college-educated members of a new generation of Indians launched public demonstrations to protest the substandard conditions on the reservations. "As far as the new activists were concerned," researcher Carl Waldman writes,

> not only had the federal government failed to fulfill the promises of its treaties, acts, and agreements in correcting the miserable Indian socioeconomic conditions, but federal officials continued to act [as if] they alone knew what was best for Indian peoples. Activists were also concerned with continuing racial discrimination in housing and employment, as well as police brutality against Indians.[68]

Among the new activist groups that addressed these problems was the American Indian Movement, established in 1968. The following year several of its members occupied Alcatraz Island in San Francisco Bay—the site of an infamous prison—to attract attention to their

A family living on Arizona's Navajo reservation occupies a small rustic house. Even today, some reservation homes lack electricity.

cause. Not long afterward, in 1972 other Native American protesters staged a demonstration they called the Trail of Broken Treaties. It consisted of a sit-in in the offices of the Bureau of Indian Affairs in Washington, DC. Still another protest widely covered by the media occurred in 1973, when several Indian and white demonstrators took control of the village of Wounded Knee, South Dakota.

These and other efforts by activists helped focus the public's and Congress's attention on Indians' long-standing grievances. As a result, US Indian policy began to change much faster than in the past. A coalition of Indian activists, government officials, and concerned citizens started pushing for better treatment of and expanded opportunities for Native Americans. Common goals included creating economic and social programs designed to raise Indians' standard of living, making efforts to revitalize traditional Indian culture, seeking ways to increase job opportunities for Indians, and promoting understanding between Indians and whites in hopes of reducing anti-Indian prejudice.

Profound Respect for the Land

Although progress toward meeting these and related goals has been made in recent years, today both Indian and white American leaders agree that much still needs to be done. As late as 2012 almost 25 percent of the residents of most reservations lived below the poverty line, 14 percent of the homes in these areas had no electricity, and nearly half of adult Indians lacked a high school diploma.

These leaders also acknowledge that achieving true equality and justice for Native Americans has been and remains a difficult, time-consuming process. This is primarily due to the enormous extent of the damages done to the tribes in the past. The devastation wrought by centuries of cruel and brutal removal and relocation programs, coupled with deeply entrenched racism, can neither easily nor quickly be erased. As Waldman points out, Indians long battled and managed to survive "against overwhelming forces"[69] that sought to destroy them.

Yet in an incredible display of fortitude and boundless courage, the Indians refused to be destroyed. They survived the attempted genocide perpetrated on them and today still maintain a remarkable degree of self-identity, pride, and sheer resolve. That mighty assault on them was driven by naked greed for their lands, physically manifested in repeated forced removals. What their oppressors did not comprehend was that a truly profound love and respect for those lands lay at the very core of Native American culture. Indians everywhere, scholar Stephen Pevar explains, had a tremendous determination "to preserve their ancestral lands and their culture, religion, and traditions, many of which were tied to those lands."[70]

Thus, although white society could remove the Indians from the land, they could not remove the land from the Indians' hearts and souls. That simple but deeply insightful and sophisticated concept is what non-Indians can learn from Indians to the benefit of both, Waldman says. "Having been deprived of most of what was once all their land," he writes, "they should be granted the necessary means to achieve their social and cultural goals." He adds that Native American culture "is a national treasure. *Its* renewal is *everyone's* renewal."[71]

Source Notes

Introduction: The Defining Characteristics of Indian Removal

1. Emmerich de Vattel, *The Law of Nations, or Principles of the Law of Nature Applied to the Conduct and Affairs of Nations and Sovereigns.* 1883 edition by Joseph Chitty. www.constitution.org.
2. Quoted in Christopher Davis, *North American Indian.* London: Hamlyn, 1969, p. 67.
3. Quoted in Diane E. Foulds, "Who Scalped Whom?," *Boston Globe,* December 12, 2000, p. B10.
4. Quoted in Penobscot Culture and History, "1755 Proclamation." www.penobscotculture.com.
5. Lenore A. Stiffarm and Phil Lane Jr., "The Demography of Native North America: A Question of Indian Survival," in *The State of Native America: Genocide, Colonization, and Resistance,* ed. M. Annette Jaimes. Boston: South End, 1992, p. 37.
6. Arrell M. Gibson, *The American Indian: Prehistory to the Present.* Toronto: Heath, 1980, p. 329.

Chapter One: What Conditions Led to Native American Relocation?

7. Quoted in Brian W. Dippie, *The Vanishing American: White Attitudes and U.S. Indian Policy.* Middletown, CT: Wesleyan University Press, 1982, p. 70.
8. Quoted in T.C. McLuhan, ed., *Touch the Earth: A Self-Portrait of Indian Existence.* New York: Promontory, 1971, p. 54.
9. Quoted in Lehigh University Digital Library, "Robert Gray's *A Good Speed to Virginia.*" http://digital.lib.lehigh.edu.

10. Quoted in Francis P. Prucha, *American Indian Policy in the Formative Years: The Indian Trade and Intercourse Acts, 1790–1834.* Cambridge, MA: Harvard University Press, 1962, p. 162.

11. Gibson, *The American Indian,* p. 250.

12. Quoted in Peter Nabokov, ed., *Native American Testimony.* New York: Harper and Row, 1978, p. 118.

13. Quoted in Nabokov, *Native American Testimony,* p. 120.

14. Quoted in Yale Law School Avalon Project, "Treaty with the Delawares, 1778," 2008. http://avalon.law.yale.edu.

15. Yale Law School Avalon Project, "Treaty with the Delawares, 1778."

16. Quoted in Anthony F.C. Wallace, *Jefferson and the Indians: The Tragic Fate of the First Americans.* Cambridge, MA: Harvard University Press, 1999, p. 165.

17. Quoted in Frederick W. Turner, ed., *The Portable North American Indian Reader.* New York: Viking, 1974, p. 247.

18. Quoted in Turner, *The Portable North American Indian Reader,* p. 246.

19. Quoted in Benjamin B. Thatcher, *Indian Biography, or an Historical Account of Those Individuals Who Have Been Distinguished Among the North American Natives as Orators, Warriors, Statesmen and Other Remarkable Characters,* vol. 2. Whitefish, MT: Kessinger, 2010, p. 237.

Chapter Two: Formulating Removal and Relocation Policy

20. Benjamin Franklin, *The Autobiography of Benjamin Franklin.* Boston: Houghton Mifflin, 1896, p. 229.

21. Carl Van Doren, *Benjamin Franklin.* New York: Penguin, 1991, p. 209.

22. Quoted in James Hall, *A Memoir of the Public Services of William Henry Harrison of Ohio.* Philadelphia: Biddle, 1836, pp. 90–91.

23. Quoted in Wallace, *Jefferson and the Indians,* p. 273.

24. Quoted in American Presidency Project, "James Monroe: Special Message, January 27, 1825." www.presidency.ucsb.edu.

25. Quoted in American Presidency Project, "James Monroe."

26. Peter Farb, *Man's Rise to Civilization as Shown by the Indians of North America from Primeval Times to the Coming of the Industrial State*. New York: Dutton, 1968, p. 300.

27. Howard Zinn, *A People's History of the United States*. New York: HarperCollins, 1980, p. 125.

28. Quoted in Turner, *The Portable North American Indian Reader*, pp. 249–50.

29. Quoted in American Presidency Project, "Andrew Jackson: Inaugural Address, March 4, 1829." www.presidency.ucsb.edu.

30. Lewis Cass, "Removal of the Indians," *North American Review*, vol. 30, 1830, pp. 70–71.

31. Henry Storrs, *Speech of Henry R. Storrs, of New York, in Committee of the Whole House, May 15, 1830*. Utica: Northway and Porter, 1830, p. 48.

32. Quoted in John Ehle, *Trail of Tears: The Rise and Fall of the Cherokee Nation*. New York: Doubleday, 1988, pp. 275–76.

33. Quoted in Ehle, *Trail of Tears*, pp. 276–77.

34. Quoted in Brian Hicks, *Toward the Setting Sun: John Ross, the Cherokees, and the Trail of Tears*. New York: Atlantic Monthly Press, 2011, p. 287.

Chapter Three: Uprooting and Relocation

35. Quoted in Gary E. Moulton, ed., *The Papers of Chief John Ross*, vol. 1. Norman: University of Oklahoma Press, 1985, pp. 211–12.

36. A.J. Langguth, *Andrew Jackson and the Trail of Tears to the Civil War*. New York: Simon and Schuster, 2010, p. 263.

37. Quoted in Moulton, *The Papers of Chief John Ross*, vol. 1, p. 88.

38. Quoted in Thurman Wilkins, *Cherokee Tragedy: The Story of the Ridge Family and the Decimation of a People*. New York: Macmillan, 1970, p. 277.

39. Alexis de Tocqueville, *Democracy in America*, vol. 1, trans. Henry Reeve, 2013. www.gutenberg.org.

40. Quoted in Arrell M. Gibson, *Oklahoma: A History of Five Centuries*. Norman: University of Oklahoma Press, 1965, p. 88.

41. Gibson, *The American Indian*, pp. 325–26.

42. Quoted in Dru J. Murray, "The Unconquered Seminoles," Florida History. www.abfla.com.

43. Quoted in Moulton, *The Papers of Chief John Ross*, vol. 1, p. 88.

44. Hicks, *Toward the Setting Sun*, p. 297.

45. James Mooney, *History, Myths, and Sacred Formulas of the Cherokees*. Fairview, NC: Bright Mountain, 1992, p. 130.

46. Quoted in Vicki Rozema, ed., *Voices from the Trail of Tears*. Winston-Salem, NC: Blair, 2003, p. 140.

47. Quoted in Ehle, *Trail of Tears*, p. 358.

48. Quoted in Mooney, *History, Myths, and Sacred Formulas of the Cherokees*, p. 130.

49. Quoted in Rozema, *Voices from the Trail of Tears*, p. 148.

Chapter Four: Problems and Suffering of the Relocated Tribes

50. Quoted in Collected State of the Union Addresses of U.S. Presidents, "Andrew Jackson, December 6, 1830." www.presidency.ucsb.edu.

51. George Catlin, "Letters and Notes on the Manners, Customs, and Conditions of North American Indians, Letter No. 9," Campfire Stories with George Catlin. http://americanart.si.edu.

52. Quoted in Arnon Gutfeld, *American Exceptionalism: The Effects of Plenty on the American Experience*. Portland, OR: Sussex Academic, 2002, p. 168.

53. Quoted in Collected State of the Union Addresses of U.S. Presidents, "Martin Van Buren, December 3, 1838." www.infoplease.com.

54. Quoted in Rachel C. Eaton, *Chronicles of Oklahoma*, vol. 8. Oklahoma City: Oklahoma Historical Society, 1930, p. 372.

55. Gibson, *The American Indian*, p. 336.

56. Quoted in Philip Weeks, *Farewell, My Nation: The American Indian and the United States, 1820–1890*. Arlington Heights, IL: Harlan Davidson, 1990, p. 58.

57. Garrick Bailey and Roberta G. Bailey, "The Civil War in Indian Territory," in *Encyclopedia of North American Indians*, ed. Frederick E. Hoxie. Boston: Houghton Mifflin, 1996, p. 125.

58. Quoted in Famous American Trials, "Little Crow." http://law2.umkc.edu.

59. Weeks, *Farewell, My Nation*, p. 47.

Chapter Five: What Is the Legacy of Native American Removal?

60. Quoted in Francis P. Prucha, ed., *Documents of United States Indian Policy*. Lincoln: University of Nebraska Press, 2000, p. 81.

61. Quoted in Henry E. Fritz, *The Movement for Indian Assimilation, 1860–1890*. Philadelphia: University of Pennsylvania Press, 1963, p. 81.

62. Quoted in Nabokov, *Native American Testimony*, p. 123.

63. Quoted in *New Perspectives on the West*, "Chief Joseph," PBS, 2001. www.pbs.org.

64. Weeks, *Farewell, My Nation*, p. 231.

65. Quoted in Lorettus S. Metcalf, *The Forum*, vol. 10. New York: Forum, 1891, p. 715.

66. Quoted in Metcalf, *The Forum*, vol. 10, p. 715.

67. Quoted in Indians.org, "Luther Standing Bear." www.indians.org.

68. Carl Waldman, *Atlas of the North American Indian*. New York: Facts On File, 1985, p. 204.

69. Waldman, *Atlas of the North American Indian*, p. 211.

70. Stephen Pevar, *The Rights of Indians and Tribes*. New York: Oxford University Press, 2012, p. 3.

71. Waldman, *Atlas of the North American Indian*, p. 211.

Important People of the Indian Relocation

Lewis Cass: Secretary of war for President Andrew Jackson, Cass helped make the case for Indian removal policies by publicly denouncing Indians as savages. The insults he hurled at the Cherokees were particularly harsh.

George Catlin: A white American painter who sympathized with the Indians' plight. He visited fifty different tribes, painted portraits of selected members of those groups, and argued in writing that Indians were both civilized and noble.

John Collier: Commissioner of Indian Affairs under President Franklin D. Roosevelt, he spearheaded the 1934 Indian Reorganization Act, which contained new, at the time more humane policies for dealing with the nation's surviving Native Americans.

Dull Knife: A prominent chief of the Cheyenne, he led his people off their designated reservation in a courageous escape attempt that ultimately failed.

Ulysses S. Grant: A leading Civil War general who later became president. He advocated a set of Indian policies that included assigning Native Americans to reservations. Together referred to as Grant's Peace Policy, these plans were widely seen as more humane than most others proposed by white leaders in the post–Civil War era.

William Henry Harrison: A white American soldier, general, politician, and future president, he led the US Army in several key battles with Indians, including the one in which Tecumseh died.

Andrew Jackson: One of the more controversial US presidents, he began as a soldier who led both whites and Indian allies against the Creeks and other eastern Indians who resisted white intrusions into their ancestral lands. After ascending to the presidency, Jackson pushed through the 1830 Indian Removal Act and demanded that the Cherokee and several other eastern tribes be relocated to the so-called Indian Territory that lay west of the Mississippi.

Thomas Jefferson: One of the US founding fathers and the new nation's third president. Among numerous other achievements, he struck the deal with France known as the Louisiana Purchase. This nearly doubled the country's size overnight and seemed to provide an area to which eastern Indian tribes might be relocated, a policy that Jefferson viewed as inevitable.

Thomas Jessup: An army general charged with the task of forcing the Florida Seminoles to give up their lands and relocate to Indian Territory. He repeatedly used deceptive, dishonorable tactics to achieve his goals.

Joseph: A famous chief of the Nez Percé tribe who led his people off their assigned reservation and onto a months-long dash for freedom beyond the Canadian border. US forces caught up to and detained the Indians when they were only a few miles from their goal.

Little Crow: A Dakota chief who warned his people, along with Indians everywhere, that whites were too numerous, deceitful, and persistent for the tribes to defeat.

James Monroe: The fifth US president. He openly stated that Indians were not civilized enough to successfully live among whites. Although he did not personally pursue Indian removal, his beliefs and remarks helped solidify the attitudes that led to that destructive policy.

James Mooney: A nineteenth-century anthropologist who conducted a detailed study that documented the removal of various eastern Indian tribes.

Osceola: Chief of the rebellious Seminoles in Florida, he resisted attempts by General Thomas Jessup to round up and relocate the resistant Seminoles. When Osceola tried to approach Jessup under a white flag, the general betrayed that international sign of truce and threw him in jail, where he died.

Hiram Price: A former commissioner of Indian Affairs, in the 1890s Price made the false case to the American public that Indians needed to be confined to reservations for their own good.

John Ridge: Among the Georgia Cherokees, he and his father, known as Major Ridge, opposed Chief John Ross and his followers and advocated agreeing with the US government's demands that the tribe relocate to Indian Territory.

John Ross: A longtime chief of the Georgia Cherokees, he led the tribe's so-called National Party, which called for strongly resisting the removal and relocation policies of Andrew Jackson and other white leaders. Ross also tried to broker a deal between the US government and the rebellious Seminole chief Osceola.

Winfield Scott: Later noted for his service in the Mexican-American War and Civil War, Scott was assigned the duty of removing the Georgia Cherokees during the winter of 1837–1838. He ordered his men to carry out the plan as gently as possible, but many of them ignored him, which led to much misery and death.

Philip H. Sheridan: A noted Civil War general who advocated that Indians be treated harshly and confined to remote reservations.

Luther Standing Bear: An Oglala Sioux, he was a leading Indian thinker, author, and actor during the early decades of the twentieth century. His books about the experiences of Indians caught the eye of US official John Collier, who asked Standing Bear to help him craft the more humane policies making up the 1934 Indian Reorganization Act.

Alexis de Tocqueville: A French intellectual, historian, and writer who traveled widely through the United States in the 1830s. A passage in his classic book, *Democracy in America*, graphically describes some of the brutalities of the Choctaw removal.

Martin Van Buren: Andrew Jackson's immediate successor in the White House, Van Buren essentially continued his predecessor's removal and relocation policies, including the forced removal of the Georgia Cherokees that culminated in the brutal Trail of Tears episode.

For Further Research

Books

Robert Forczyk, *Nez Perce, 1877: The Last Fight*. Oxford, UK: Osprey, 2013.

Brian Hicks, *Toward the Setting Sun: John Ross, the Cherokees, and the Trail of Tears*. New York: Atlantic Monthly Press, 2011.

Laurie C. Hillstrom, *Defining Moments: American Indian Relocation and the Trail to Wounded Knee*. Chicago: KWS, 2011.

Sue Vander Hook, *Trail of Tears*. Minneapolis: Abdo, 2010.

Frederick Hoxie, *This Indian Country: American Indian Activists and the Place They Made*. New York: Penguin, 2012.

A.J. Langguth, *Andrew Jackson and the Trail of Tears to the Civil War*. New York: Simon and Schuster, 2010.

Russell M. Lawson, *Encyclopedia of American Indian Issues*. 2 Vols. Westport, CT: Greenwood, 2013.

Stew Magnuson, *Wounded Knee 1973: Still Bleeding; The American Indian Movement, the FBI, and Their Fight to Bury the Sins of the Past*. Omaha, NE: Courtbridge, 2013.

James H. Malone, *The Chickasaw Nation: A Short Sketch of a Noble People*. New York: Createspace, 2013.

David W. Miller, *The Taking of American Indian Lands in the Southeast: A History of Territorial Cessions and Forced Relocations, 1607–1840*. Jefferson, NC: McFarland, 2011.

Michael Oberg, *Native America: A History*. New York: Wiley-Blackwell, 2010.

Robert O'Neill and Charles M. Robinson, *Battle on the Plains: The United States Plains Wars*. New York: Rosen, 2011.

Theda Perdue, *Native American Indians: A Very Short Introduction*. New York: Oxford University Press, 2010.

Stephen Pevar, *The Rights of Indians and Tribes*. New York: Oxford University Press, 2012.

William R. Sanford, *Nez Perce Chief Joseph*. Berkeley Heights, NJ: Enslow, 2013.

Internet Sources

History Channel, "Trail of Tears." www.history.com/topics/trail-of-tears.

Our Documents, "Transcript of President Andrew Jackson's Message to Congress on Indian Removal." www.ourdocuments.gov/doc.php?flash=true&doc=25&page=transcript.

PBS, "Indian Removal, 1814–1858." www.pbs.org/wgbh/aia/part4/4p2959.html.

Websites

Andrew Jackson, History Channel (www.history.com/topics/andrew-jackson). A well-written brief overview of the life of Andrew Jackson, including his participation in the wars against the Creek Indians and his role in Indian removal while president.

Chief Joseph, *New Perspectives on the West*, PBS (www.pbs.org/weta/thewest/people/a_c/chiefjoseph.htm). A general look at the trials and accomplishments of one of the greatest and most famous American Indian leaders.

Early Native American Literature (http://nativeamericanwriters.com /index.html). This site offers valuable information about some of the more important nineteenth-century Indian writers, including some who experienced or observed removal and relocation of various tribes.

Indian Affairs, US Department of the Interior (www.bia.gov/FAQs). This excellent site sponsored by the US Bureau of Indian Affairs provides valuable information about the status of American Indians today, including an official definition of an Indian tribe, the current relationship between the US government and the Indian tribes, how the tribal governments are organized and operate, the size of the Native American population, how the Bureau of Indian Affairs works, and much more.

Indian Removal Act, Library of Congress (www.loc.gov/rr/program /bib/ourdocs/Indian.html). This excellent online source provides an overview of the act, links to other sites with relevant information, and a list of books and articles to consult.

Index

of Choctaws, 45
of Creeks, 47
of Tecumseh, 27, 32
Wounded Knee (1890), 74
Delawares, treaty with, 25
diseases, 12, 66
Dull Knife (chief of the Cheyennes), 65,
66, 73
Dustin, Hannah, 12

eastern United States
area of Louisiana Purchase for Indians
in, 34
coexistence of whites and Indians,
30–32, 34, 36
completion of removal, 53, 54
Creek treaty, 36
Indian Removal Act and, 37–38
population, 29
self-removal, 35
settlers' expansion in, 15–16
extinction, relocation as preventing
Indians', 34

Farb, Peter, 36
Florida, 47–49, **48**
Fox (Meskwaki), 22, 35
Franklin, Benjamin, 30
French trappers, 22

genocide, 13
Georgia
relocation of Cherokees from
Indian Removal Act passage, 37–38
pressure to leave, 38
Ross's actions, 41–43
support for Cherokee, 40
ultimatum from Jackson, 39, 40
relocation of Creek from, 36, 45–47
Ghost Dance, 73–74
Gibson, Arrell M.
on Border Indians, 60
on measures to force Indians to cede
land, 46–47
on severity of removal, 13
on treatment of Indians after American
Revolution, 23
gold in California, 60–62, **61**
Grant, Ulysses S., 68, 70

Gray, Robert, 19
Great Spirit, 17, 18
greed of white settlers, 11

Harrison, William Henry, 31–32
Hicks, Brian, 49

Indian Intercourse Act (1834), 35
Indian Removal Act (1830), 8, 37–38, **56**
Indian Reorganization Act (1934), 75–76,
77
Indians
cultural regions, 31
current conditions, 77, **78**, 79
differences with white settlers, 15–17
possibility of coexistence with settlers,
30–32, 34, 36
relationship to land, 17, 76, 79
religious beliefs of, 18
See also views of Indians *under* white
settlers
Indian Territory/Country
boundaries of, 35
Cherokees in, 60
Civil War in, 62–64
clashes between tribes, 59–60
trails across, 60–61
US government promises about, 58
white settlers in, 65
Iowas, 59–60

Jackson, Andrew
background of, 36
on necessity of removal, 55
ultimatum to Cherokee, 39, 40
views on Indians, 36–37
Jamestown, Virginia
aid from Indians, 15
Powhatan opposition to expansion of,
20, 22, 24
whites' arrival at, **16**
Jefferson, Thomas
forced removal and, 35
Louisiana Purchase, 32, 34, 37
on nature of treaties, 25
on westward expansion, 26
Jesup, Thomas, 48, 49
Joseph (chief of the Nez Percés), 17, 73

Picture Credits

Cover: © Christie's Images/Corbis

Album/Prisma/Newscom: 10

Katrin Azimi: 56

© Bettmann/Corbis: 37, 76

© Corbis: 64, 71

© Currier & Ives Print of Californ/PoodlesRock/Corbis: 61

© W. Langdon Kihn/National Geographic Society/Corbis: 44

Picture History/Newscom: 52

Thinkstock images: 6, 7

© Alison Wright/National Geographic Society/Corbis: 78

Steve Zmina: 31

Landing at Jamestown, 1607 (colour litho), English School, (17th century)/Private Collection/The Bridgeman Art Library: 16

The massacre of the settlers in 1622, plate VII, from 'America, Part XIII', German edition, 1628 (coloured engraving), Merian, Matthaus, the Elder (1593–1650)/Virginia Historical Society, Richmond, Virginia, USA/The Bridgeman Art Library: 24

Osceola in Captivity, c. 1837 (oil on canvas), Eastman, Captain Seth (1808–75)/Private Collection/The Bridgeman Art Library: 48

About the Author

Historian and award-winning author Don Nardo has published numerous books for young people about American history. They include comprehensive studies of the founding fathers and their writings, US political institutions, several of America's wars, the Great Depression, and Native American history and culture. Nardo, who also composes and arranges orchestral music, lives with his wife, Christine, in Massachusetts.